WOMEN IN NORTH-EAST INDIA:
An Annotated Bibliography

WOMEN IN NORTH-EAST INDIA

An Annotated Bibliography

Compiled & Edited by

C. KHONGLAH

AKANSHA PUBLISHING HOUSE

NEW DELHI-110002 (INDIA)

AKANSHA PUBLISHING HOUSE
4649-B/21, Ansari Road
Darya Ganj, New Delhi - 110 002
Ph.: 23263193 / 9811582579 / 09435116718
Fax: 011-23263193
Email: ektabooks@yahoo.com

Women in North-East India: An Annotated Bibliography

First Published 2008
ISBN 978-81-8370-120-4

PRINTED IN INDIA

Published by Akansha Publishing House, New Delhi and Printed at Aryan Enterprises, Delhi.

CONTENTS

FOREWORD

The status and the issues related to women in North-East India has been discussed and debated in the various academic forums for a long time. However, till date there is no concrete effort made to provide a documentation of the works done on women in North-East India.

Considering the need in this direction, Ms. Cerilla Konglah, our colleague in the Centre, made an effort to compile a state-wise annotated bibliography on women in North-East India.

We would like to put on record our appreciation to Ms Konglah, Documentation Officer, ICSSR-NERC for compiling the entire volume with the assistance of other staff in the Centre.

Indeed, it gives us immense satisfaction to place before the academic community and the general public *Women in North-East India: An Annotated Bibliography*.

We hope scholars and users will find this volume useful and informative.

C JOSHUA THOMAS
Acting Director

ICSSR-NERC
Shillong

PREFACE

The Indian Council of Social Science Research of North Eastern Regional Centre (ICSSR-NERC), Shillong (1977), has brought out Eight Bibliographies on Social Science on North East in mimeograph form since its inception. The present annotated bibliography is the first venture of the Documentation Unit of our Centre on Women Studies in North East India. The main aim of this volume is to provide a useful reference tool to scholars interested on the issue under reference.

The bibliography contains Seminars on Status of Women and other women related issues presented during the workshops and conferences organized by various Literary and Research Organisations of the seven States under the auspices of the ICSSR-NERC. Books on Women in North East also are included for the benefit of the scholars working on this area of study. This bibliography is divided into seven parts:

Part I. Status of Women

Part II. Women and Education

Part III. Women and Urbanization

Part IV. Women and Development

Part V. Women and 73rd Amendment Act, 1992

Part VI. Papers on Women in Proceedings of North East India History Association

Part VII. Books on Women in North East

Part VIII. Monographs.

The entries in the bibliography are arranged State-wise. Every entry is provided with an annotation, so that scholars, looking for his/her work of interest may be able to get a general idea about its coverage. Further, the author index is also included in the Appendix arranged in alphabetical order for prompt access of the scholars to the right information without wasting their time.

Many of the works done on *Women in North East* are not included in our present effort in view of the constraint that we have to include only the seminars/ conferences/workshops proceedings and a few books available in our library collection. We apologize for the inconvenience. However, we hope to be of more service in future. We also invite suggestions from our users.

Lastly, this bibliography would not have been brought out in its present form without the keen interest taken by our Director, Dr C.J. Thomas and the support of our team work particularly Mr Romauldo M. Pasi, who deserve a special thanks for silently doing his work on the computer. This acknowledgement would be incomplete if we do not thank Ms Iamon M. Syiem, Head, Department of Sociology, St. Edmund's College, Shillong who has gone through the typescript and offered the valuable suggestions.

On this occasion, we also remember our colleagues, (L) Mrs Jean Mebari Blah and (L) Mr Bantiplang Nongkhlaw for their urgrudging help towards the project in the initial phase.

CERILLA KHONGLAH

Documentation Officer

INTRODUCTION

Women issues have become an area of interest among the researchers in the field of social sciences. Studies on various issues related to women reflect that nearly half of the world's population constitute of women. Their contribution in different fields is highly appreciated. Unfortunately, women are still being suppressed and oppressed in different forms of social, economic and political spheres in many parts of the world. Consequent to the discrimination and marginalization of women in the society have also become the issue of debate among social scientists, researchers, social reformers, planners and women activists at different levels particularly at the international level.

Under the initiative of the United Nations to improve the status of women, the World Conference on *Women* held in different places during 1975-1995 witnessed the solidarity of the half of the world's population. Organizing themselves at the international level, women took a pledge to share their problems and fight for justice. On the direction of United Nations, studies on the *Status of Women* were conducted world-wide as agenda on *Women Issues* for the *First World Conference in* 1975 held at Mexico the year declared as *Women' International Year* aiming at achieving universal equality, integration in the social, economic and political spheres as well as to maintain international peace. The Conference was the first landmark in the history of the United Nations where implementation of the *Plan of Action* was then dwelt at length resulted to the constitution of the Committee on the *Elimination of Discrimination Against Women of the United Nations (CEDAW)*. This Report entitled, *The Work of CEDAW*, 1982-86 was published by United Nations from New York in 1989. The Programme of Action was discussed at the 2nd *World Conference on Women* held at Copenhagen in 1980, while *Nairobi Conference in* 1985 observed a decade of United Nations on women led to the emergence of the *Forward Looking Strategies* to observe as the agenda issues for the next decade of its activities. It is heartening to note that during the *United Nations Decade on Women*, participants made numerous recommendations, designed to rectify the imbalance. In the Report of World Conference of the *United Nations Decade of Women* held in Nairobi in 1985, *resolutions were passed stressing on the need for political parties to nominate women candidates and give them real chance of winning elections for government and non-governmental organizations to educate women about their own often newly-won civil, political and social rights. Participants also voiced support for time tables and quotas to set concrete goal for increasing the participation of women.*[1] The movement had made a herculean task at the international level during the two decades formulating plans and policies to elevate female population widely. However, without the regional and national cooperation of the member governments, this movement would not have reached its height. Therefore, in South Asia, it may be noted that under the initiative of the SAARC, in pursuance of the decision of the first meeting of its Council of Ministers, a *Technical Committee* on *Women Development* was formed in October 1986.[2] *Meeting periodically, the Committee organizes workshops, training programmes, exhibitions, study tours etc. Exchange of information and data on women, preparation of bibliographies, directories, etc. are also facilitated.* Further to strengthen women's initiative, the Asian and Pacific Centre for Women of the UN ESCAP known as the Women's Information Network for Asia and Pacific was set up to improve availability and accessibility of data and information needed by Government policy makers and to promote and monitor the effective participation of women in all aspects of national development. But one of the most remarkable decisions of the international level was taken at the workshop on leadership held at Bangalore in which the Groots South Asia International was announced as a network of NGO's working in SAARC countries. *The ambitious agenda for action includes fostering grassroots and regional networking, information exchange, leadership development* etc.[3] Interestingly, the SAARC Conference on Women was held in Shillong too in 1986.

Women in India

Being concerned at the plight of women in India, Sarala Gopalan[4] has rightly remarked that *"We have traveled a long way from the First UN World Conference on Women in Mexico in* 1975 *to the Fourth World Conference at Beijing in* 1995 *in search of Equality, Development and Peace".* True, it has been a long journey for UN women in search of justice, yet under the network of the women's world wide web (WWWW) brought home of the participating nations including India the fruit of success at the setting up of the *National and State*

Commissions for Women in their respective countries and states to address the problems and grievances of women. India as one of the signatories of the United Nations has also set up the National Commission for Women under the National Commission, Act 1992. But as discussed we should not forget that women in our country are still the victims of suppression and exploitation of the society.

It is said that, women in the Vedic period participated in all fields like men and took active part in every sphere of human life. Woman was man's best friend, his co-worker and never his inferior; she had enjoyed the property rights, discussed political and social problems and took part in all religious activities. There was no bar on the marriage of widows or women remaining unmarried. But with the passage of time women in India have to face the brunt of various problems of the social processes like *purdah* system, polygamy, child marriage, *sati*, dowry, and female foeticide, deprivation of education and property rights. Nevertheless, women did not shy away from taking part in any movement for the good cause as and when called for. One of such is their participation in the national freedom movement during the colonial period. Women from different corners of the country irrespective of their ethnic identity came out of their traditional four walls in response to the call to show their solidarity, courage and sacrifice in saving their motherland, India from the clutches of the alien rulers. The contribution of women was then recognized not only economically but also of their glaring participation in the freedom movement, that, without half of the country's population participation *India's Independence* would not have been achieved. Therefore, the post-Independence era saw the setting up of the Central Social Welfare Board in 1953, the first landmark in the history of the *First Five Year Plan* (1951-56) of the Government of free India a concern for women's welfare orientation. Another landmark in the history of India is the inclusion of the chapter on *Women and Development* in the *Sixth Five Year Plan* (1980-85). The next landmark in the history of women's welfare and development was the appointment in 1971 of a *Committee* on *Status of Women* under the Chairmanship of Mrs Phulrenu Guha to examine all the rights and status of women in the context of changing social and economic conditions in the country and problems relating to the advancement of women.

The major outcome of this report was the National Plan of Action, 1976 (Vats, 2004).[5] We further saw the passing of the Constitution 73rd Amendment Act, 1993 considering 30% reservation for women in Panchayati Raj Institutions. There are also a number of resolutions taken from time to time at the international and regional cooperation *Conferences on Women* of the participating countries of the United Nations towards uplift of women. One of such decision is to disseminate information on women issues. In India besides formulations of policies and developmental programmes for women in the Five Year Plans, especially, after the publication of the Report in 1974, on *Women Towards Equality,* with a focus to improve the conditions of Indian women not only in the field of education, health, nutrition but also to meet the need of women in the development of the society. Thus, to collect and disseminate information related to the development of women, *Women and Development Studies Information Networks* were set up in the country by several academic/research institutions particularly in the late 80s. Similarly networking among *Women's*

Development Corporations and *Women Studies Centres* were also initiated by clearing house for Information of Women's Division of NIPCCD. Perhaps it is not out of place to say that in India particularly for more than three decades now that is from 1975, the *International Women's Year* onwards women must have seen as the most productive period in the history of women's welfare, development and empowerment, with regard to the flow of information on women issues and formulation of policies and development programmes for women, such as the *National Policy for Empowerment of Women, 2001*, the introduction of the *Protection of Women from Domestic Violence, 2006, Fast Track Court* and many other programmes and schemes for economic and social welfare of women. During this period, we also observed the active organization of various awareness programmes on women issues in different parts of the country by interested organizations including women organizations.

As mentioned earlier, women in India, be it in the North, in the South, in the West or in the East or in the Eastern most part of the country are not free from different types of harassment, gender prejudice or gender bias in different spheres of life. However, women should not feel that they are being marginalized in the society, but, to strive to achieve their goal in this world of *survival of the fittest*.

Coming to North East India, the region comprises of the States of Arunachal Pradesh, Assam, Meghalaya, Mizoram, Nagaland and Tripura known as the *'Seven Sisters'* having diverse ethnic groups, speaking different languages, having different history, traditions, costumes and beliefs. Geographically, the region is almost isolated from the rest of the country being surrounded by Bangladesh, Bhutan, and Burma (now Myanmar) and China connected by a narrow corridor between the Himalayas on the one side and Bangladesh on the other. The Region is less known to different parts of the country except on some occasion when some news flashed through the print and electronic media. As such information on condition of women in this part of the country is also less known to those interested on this issue. It is a fact that women in North-East India are enjoying a better position in the society particularly the tribal women compared to their counterparts in the rest of the country in the absence of social evils like dowry, infanticide and *sati*. However, we cannot deny the fact that women in North-East have to face various social and economic problems such as illiteracy, poverty, landlessness, poor health, alcoholism, drugs, broken homes, eve teasing, domestic violence, single parent, early marriage, gender discrimination of wage, discrimination of democratic participation in decision-making at the grassroot/ traditional institutions at the cost of the customary laws, discouragement of participation in electoral politics, so on and so forth. The present situation in the region, the peace-loving people of North-East are being disturbed with various types of problems in the society like, unrest, violence, armed conflict, ethnic conflict, terrorism, insurgency, law and order, extortion, etc. These are some of the factors affecting normal life in the region. In such a situation, it is quite obvious that women and children are always the first to be affected in the society. So, the problems of women in North-East are no less different from other women in the rest of the country.

However, generally speaking studies on women in North-East till the late '80s were very limited and those available are scattered in different sources. Therefore, the North Eastern Regional Centre of the Indian Council of Social Science Research, set up in 1977 in Shillong to promote social science in North-East India sponsored and organized a number of workshops, seminars, symposia, annual lecture series in the field of social science research in North-East including issues on women right from its inception. As mentioned, papers presented during the above programmes are maintained in the Library and Documentation Analysis Unit of the NERC-ICSSR. Some of the proceedings of the same are published in book forms by the organizers. With the increasing interest of the scholars on the issue under reference, today, we witness the flow of research works on women in North-East not only those sponsored and organized by the Centre but with the sponsorship from other sources extended to quite a number of individuals, Professional Organizations, Departments in the Universities, Colleges, and many others to conduct such research programmes in this field of study.

As one of the objectives of the North Eastern Regional Centre of the Indian Council of Social Science Research, is to render bibliographical and documentation service for research work, the present annotated bibliography on *Women Studies in North-East India* is therefore an attempt to facilitate scholars, social activists, policy makers, and students to get their needed information on women without much difficulty.

NOTES AND REFERENCES

1. Ranjana Kumari (Ed), *Women in Decision Making,* Vikas Publishing House, New Delhi, 1992, p.9.
2. Hema Balasubramaniam, *Networking for Strengthening Women's Power at National and SAARC Levels,* in Ranjana Kumar (Ed), *op.cit.,* p. 97.

3. *Ibid.*
4. Sarala Gopalan, Foreword, in *Report of the Women and Child Development,* Ministry of Human Resource Development, Government of India, New Delhi, 1995.
5. Sorojini Vats, *Women's Participation in Rural Development,* Abhijeet Publications, Delhi, 2004, pp. 49-50.
6. Cerilla Khonglah, *An Introductory Note* presented during the Seminar on Women, Peace and Development: With Special Reference to Meghalaya, held in Shillong, 2000 (unpublished).

1

ARUNACHAL PRADESH

STATUS OF WOMEN IN ARUNACHAL PRADESH

A seminar on *"Status of Women in Arunachal Pradesh"* organised by the Department of Political Science, Arunachal University in collaboration with Jawaharlal Nehru College, Pasighat, was held on February 3-4, 1989. Mr. Jagin Singh, Deputy Commissioner, East Siang District, Government of Arunachal Pradesh, Professor C.L. Anand, Vice-Chancellor of Arunachal University and Chairman of the Seminar, Dr. A.C. Talukdar, Seminar Director addressed the inaugural session. In three academic business sessions, chaired by Professor C.L. Anand, Dr. J Nath and Dr. P S Datta respectively, 16 papers were presented.

Phukan, J and B N Phukan, *Status of Women in Nishi Society*

The position and status of women in any society is always determined by its socio-economic background and social customs. This is the same with the women in the Nishi society. Studying the status of women in Nishi society, the work traces the history of the Nishi people living in the hilly and difficult terrains of Arunachal Pradesh facing a hard life. The Nishis had a hard life, with jhuming as the main means of livelihood and other allied activities like rearing of livestocks and food gathering.

Choudhury, J N. *Status of Women in Pre-Literate Arunachal Society: In the Light of Social Science*

This paper attempts to analyse the question of the status of women in general and the problem of women in Arunachali society in particular. Before analyzing the status of women in Arunachal in the field of agriculture and inheritance, the author discusses the history of human existence on earth and extensively examines the status of women in pre-literate societies of the Adi, Apatani, Nishi, Monpas and Hill Miri of Aka tribes. The author is of the opinion that the Arunachal society was predominantly patriarchal and the inheritance followed the paternal line. Further, he discussed the prevalence of the institution of 'bride price', the two different forms of 'marriage by exchange' and 'marriage by purchase', as well as polygamy and divorce.

Satpathy, B. *The Changing Phenomena: A Study of Women in Arunachal Pradesh*

This paper provides a theoretical approach in determining the status of women. It points out the insignificant enforcement of legal and legislative sanction in uplifting the status of women. It discusses about their social acceptance by the society and referred to the opinion of the social anthropologist, Ralph Linton (1936). It discusses the cultural and biological factors in bringing up boys and girls in different societies. It raises some questions on equal rights to women. The need to encourage birth rate is also discussed. Also refers to women's participation in socio-economic, cultural and political fields in India, which adversely affected the variation of sex ratio as reflected in the 1961-1981 Census Report of India. The maternal mortality rate in India is another aspects discussed in this work. The observation is that there is an improvement in the status of women in Arunachal Pradesh in respect of their economic, political, cultural and social participation. The improvement of literacy rate reflected in 1961-1981 indicates a change in the status of women in the state. It comments on the laudable cooperation of educated women and the government machinery to upgrade the status of women.

Nath, Jogendra. *Status of Women in Traditional Adi Society*

Gives a brief comparative study of women in Adi society with women in Indian societies and Western cultures. Examines the position of women as depicted in Adi mythology. The practice of polyandry and polygamy in the Adi society is also discussed.

Borah, Bimal. *Gaps and Variance in Tribal Society of Arunachal Pradesh*

Outlines some of the forces and factors responsible for social change in the tribal society of Arunachal leading to the emergence of gaps and variance among them. Further observes the deprivation of women from taking part in the traditional administrative institution including the negative attitude towards improvement of their position as–cobread earner in the family.

Bormudoi, Anjali. ***Status of Women in Arunachal Pradesh***

The author discusses the status of women on the basis of various indicators reflected in the socio-cultural aspects of the tribal society in Arunachal Pradesh and also from the works of selected writers.

Choudhury, Abhijit. ***Woman's Right in Arunachal Pradesh: Customary Law to Civil Law (A Case Study)***

Discusses a court case of a girl from Gallong area who refused to go to the boy's house even while his parents had taken the bride-price. This resulted in the transfer of the customary law to the civil law.

Nyori, T. ***The Position of Women in Adi Traditional Society***

Discusses the position of women in the patriarchal and patrilineal system of the Adi society. It also gives an interpretation of polyandry and polygamy practice which is rare occurrence in the Adi society. Highlights some of the restrictions imposed on the women. Finally asserts the better position of the Adi women as compared to any other society in the country in general.

Rubok, Talom. ***The Tradition and Customary Status of Women among the Tribes of Arunachal Pradesh in General and the Adi in Particular***

Attempts to highlight the factors responsible for restrictions and limitations or the improving of the positions of Adi women before education became open to all. Observes the present changes taking place with the economic, social and political participation of women in the society.

Jamoh, Yanung. ***Status of Women in Adi Society with particular reference to Miniyong Sub-Tribe of Arunachal Pradesh***

Highlights the commendable participation of Adi women from the household chores to the ploughing of the field. Discusses the constraints faced by women in early marriage, divorce, arranged-marriage, bride-price, re-marriage of divorcees and widows. Comments on the attitudinal changes of the parents towards better upbringing of their daughters in the present day society. Finally, observes the competitive aspiration of the Adi girls in various higher studies and professions.

Saikia, Jogayamaya K K. ***Status of Women in Arunachal Pradesh- A Prospective View***

Points out the factors reflecting the status of male and female members in every society–socially, economically, academically etc. Outlines strategies in education and economic participation to promote the position of women in Arunachal Pradesh. Finally advocates for motivation of women to take up trainings in various fields.

Dutta, Parul. ***Status of Women in Arunachal Pradesh***

Gives a geographical and historical background of Arunachal Pradesh in a nutshell. Discusses the status of women under the broad headings of socio-cultural, economic, political and religious aspects.

Bhattacharjee, Tarun. ***The Status of Women in Arunachal Pradesh***

Highlights the heavy responsibility women have in

the family. Discusses the problems of women relating to bride-price, property rights, restrictions from taking part in decision-making, political and religious functions in the society. Finally, expresses hope of reformation of the social system that women may get due recognition with the spread of education.

Datta Choudhury, K. ***Change in Women in Arunachal Pradesh as observed in Three Decades***

In the light of his association with the people of Arunachal Pradesh during his service from 1957, the author presents his personal observations on the role of women in the Adi society. He discusses the engagement of women in household activities and the field and their limited access to education. The spread of education and the changing attitude towards women's education in the later period and their active political participation in the society is also discussed.

Jha, S D. ***Status of Women in Arunachal Pradesh***

Attempts to study the status of women in the light of two variables, duties and rights. Traces the history of some women celebrities during the Paranoic era, Buddhist era, and women scholars of the 14th and 15th century. Highlights the exertion of women during the freedom struggle in India. Projects the leadership of late Indira Gandhi as a woman Prime Minister, the passing of various legislations in favour of women's protection and rights. Gives a critical assessment on the deterioration of the position of women in India resulting out of foreign invasion and other forces. Dealing with Arunachal Pradesh, the author makes a historical study of all the major tribes in the state with an observation on the position of women considering their social, economic, cultural, political participations and restrictions imposed on them. Lastly, raises the question of the implementation of various Acts which were not implemented in the true spirit of protection against various atrocities, exploitation of women, property rights to women, child marriage and others.

Sermon, Kiang. ***Status of Women in Singphos Society—A Note.***

Elaborates the political, economic and religious status of Singpho women. Further, discusses the role of women in marriage ceremonies, their participation in cultural activities as well as girl's education in Singphos society.

2

ASSAM

STATUS OF WOMEN IN NON-TRIBAL SOCIETIES OF ASSAM

Status of Women in Non-Tribal Societies of Assam: Organised by the Department of History, Dibrugarh University held on October 4-5, 1988. Dr. Yosodhara Bagchi, Professor of English and Director of Women's Studies, Jadavpur University graced the seminar as the Chief Guest. A book exhibition on Women's Studies also marked the occasion.

Papers presented in the seminar have come in a book form entitled, *Status of Women in Assam with Special Reference to Non-Tribal Societies,* edited by Dr. (Mrs) S L Baruah, (New Delhi, Omsons Publications, 1992, 160p). The book contains the Editor's note with a review of each paper and an index.

Sherfuddin, Farida. ***Status of Women in the Assamese Society***

Traces the status of women in the pre-Islamic society of Arabia. The present position of women in the Assamese society as envisaged in the Islamic law is also discussed. Outlines the factors affecting the progress of women. Clarifies the meaning of the *"Purdah"* in the Muslim society. Lauds the contributions made by women economically and culturally in the society. Expresses the problems of the girl-child particularly when they attain the marriageable age. Defines the three divisions of the Muslim society in Assam. Finally, observes the equal status of Assamese Muslim women with other women in non-tribal societies of Assam.

Gogoi Nath, Jahnabi. ***Social Attitude towards Women in Medieval Assam***

Discusses the status of women in the Varna-jati society during medieval period citing references from the Vaishnava literature and other works of Yogini Tantra.

Barua, Deepali. ***Social Status of Working Women in the Assamese Society***

Gives the definition of the word *'status'* and *'role'*. Notes the discrimination of working women in a male-dominated society of Assam. Further, elaborates various challenges face by women in the society. Emphasizes on equal rights to women irrespective of caste or creed. Appeals to all working women to exert themselves in their respective responsibilities so as to receive their due recognition in the society.

Saikia, Anuva. ***Economic Status of Women in the Rural Areas of Assam***

This paper attempts to examine the factors influencing economic status of women. Views women as an integral section of every society. States that economic status of women is determined by the role played by them in economic and non-economic activities in the society. Studies the participation of rural women in economic activities in Assam, referring to the nature of work which women are undertaking in agricultural activities. Suggests measures for raising economic status of women in rural areas through proper implementation of the rural development programmes such as IRDP, TRYSEM, DWCRA etc. Stresses on generation of employment avenues and income opportunities for rural women in agricultural and allied sectors, in non-farming sectors like food processing industries, handloom and handicrafts, sericulture and household industries. Further, suggests for identification of the actual beneficiaries among women in rural areas for implementing various employment generation schemes. Lastly, pleads for setting up of training facilities for women and motivate them to take up self-employment schemes.

Saikia, P D. *Economic and Social Status of Rural Women (Non-Tribal) in Assam– A Case Study*

Draws the vital role of women in patrilineal societies as the key factor in the process of change and development. Traces the role of women in traditional societies of Asia and Africa. Highlights the economic participation of women in Islamic countries, Latin America, Sri Lanka, India, South East Asian countries, tribal Africa and Europe. Analyses the economic contribution of rural women in India. Studies the position of Assam's women. Explores a case study of the social and economic status of women in Charigaon and Kamar Bandha Gohaingoan villages. Outlining the social status of women and the nature of work that rests in the hands of women, reveals the negative attitude towards women in different aspects of life. Observes changes in the society with the spread of education.

Baruah, M Pathak and N Borthakur. ***A Study on Buying Habits and Practices of the Women Consumers of Assam***

Investigates the marketing behaviour of women in the Department of Home Management, College of Home Sciences, AAU, Jorhat covering the areas, (a) Socioeconomic background, (b) Status of women consumers in the market, (c) Buying habits of women consumers, (d) Underlying motives of decision-making in selection of non-food items, and (e) Buying behaviour of women consumers towards some marketing practices.

Hazarika, Karabi Deka. ***Status of Assamese Women in the Family and Society as reflected in Assamese Literature***

Gives a theoretical aspect of Assamese women in the family and the society as depicted in Samkaradeva's *Rukmuni Harana, Jhumaras* of Mahadeva in Ram-Navami the drama which highlighted the problem of widow remarriage, the works of Lakshminath Bezbarua, Rudai and Bhadari drawing the status of Assamese women in the family and society, and the role of rural women as tolerant and devoted wives. This paper also presents the power and authority of women in aristocratic families as reflected in the novels of Rajanikanta Bordoloi and in the drama of Jyotiprasad, Karengar Ligiri and on the other hand, the victimization of women at the cost of the rigid system of the social customs described in *Jivanar Batat* of Beena Barua, *Datal Hatir Unve Khea Randa* of Mamoni Raichan Goswami, stories and novels of Nirupama Borgohain and Sneha Devi. The author also refers to the works in Assamese literature in which a woman is glorified as loving mother, wife and daughter. The suppression and discrimination of women portrayed in the novels of Homen Borgahain, *Subala* and *Bibbinna* and in *Jiva Jarirghat* of Abdul Malik is also dwelt on. Finally, the author observes the changing attitude among the literate women in the Assamese modern society and the trend of the Assamese literature focusing on change.

Phukan, Minoti. *Status of Labour Women in the Tea Gardens of Assam*

Analyses the role of the tea garden labourer woman as wife, mother and working woman. The present study conducts a research work in the tea gardens of Upper Assam districts. Investigating the role of this particular group of women, the author highlights the participation of young girls in running the family, in looking after the younger siblings to make it convenient for the working mothers to attend to their works in the absence of creches. It investigates the non-cooperation of men-folks in management of the household works considering the heavy responsibilities women bear besides their heavy workload in the tea-garden. Further discusses the disparity of wage between male and female workers. It also focuses on the lack of recreational activities for tea labour women. Finally raises the question of educating and disciplining the children of the tea garden labourers who are deprived of any facilities as the mothers are illiterate and have no time for their children because of their heavy workload.

Sengupta, Santanu. ***Women and Religion: The Status of Assamese Women in Religion***

Presents a historical background of the position of women depicted in the Vedic and Rigveda literature. The emergence of prostitution in India is also discussed. Discusses the contact of different religions and cultures in Assam from early period. Further analyses the position of women portrayed in various religious literatures and the teachings of Sankaredva and Vaishnavas.

Mahanta, Aparna Dutta. ***Women, Religion and Science in the Non-Tribal Society in Assam***

Discusses the role of religion in an agricultural society like India. In discussing the role of religion among the non-tribal women of Assam, the author referred to the history of the people of Assam from time immemorial. Further traces the role of religion in Assam in relation to women in tribal society. Points out the importance of agriculture in the society and the participation of women therein. Highlights the role of women in religion depicted in the drama, *Rukmini Haran* and in the famous story of *Katha-Gura Charit.*

Borah, Bibha. ***Women in Administration and Politics in Medieval Assam***

Borah defines the status of women on the basis of economic condition, attitude of the society, social and religious sanctions and the awareness of their own rights. The author also analyses the role of religion in Hindu society in determining the status of women. Further, observes the advantage of the society being influenced by the tribal background of Morans, Buranjis, Chutiyas, Kacharis, Kochs and the

Jayantiyas, the social values of this background is believed to have been enjoyed by the women of the non-tribal societies of Assam. The impact of these values can be seen in the nonexistence of female infanticide, the practice of *'sati'* or child marriage and the prohibition of widow re-marriage. The author also discusses the participation of women in administration and politics. Highlights the active role played by the queens and Rajmaos in administration and politics, the participation of princesses, court-ladies, wives of nobles and many maid servants of the royal family in the *'Konwar Bidroh'*, a revolt on the dethronement of King Lakshisigha during Moamarya rule. The role played by the queens and female attendants during the plot to usurp the throne of the Koch King after the death of King Biswa Singha is dealt with. The end of freedom of women during the Burmese wars is also discussed. The author observes the change in the position of Assamese women in the 19th century when the intellectuals including Gunabhiram and Hem Chandra Barua advocated sympathy to the women in spite of the unfavourable attitude from the male chauvinism writers. Further, observes the direction of change with the launching of freedom movement when Assamese women responded to the call of the *'Father of the Nation'*. Lastly, while arguing on the rights being enjoyed by women in administration and politics, the author questioned the traditional social and religious constraints towards the uplift of women in non-tribal society in Assam.

Sharma, Dipti. ***Women of Brahmaputra Valley in the Freedom Struggle (1921-47)***

Discusses the active participation of women of Brahmaputra Valley during the freedom movement in India. Expresses disappointment on the discrimination of women identified in this work who laid down their lives during the movement.

Dutta, N W. *Political Status of Women in Assam since Independence*

Analyses the political participation of women in Assam as voters and candidates contesting in various elections to Lok Sabha and in the State Assembly since Independence to 1985. The article provides tables of year-wise distribution of the electorate showing male/female and the total number of voters in various Assembly Elections.

Borkataky, Anju. *Women and Violence in Non-tribal Societies of Assam*

Gives the definition of '*violence*'. Discussing the victimization and suppression of women in the Assamese patrilineal society, the author analyses violence on women within the family, violence on women in society, violence on women in the State, women's struggle against violence and women's participation in violence. In conclusion, asserting the role of women in violence as a struggling force, the author rejects the opinion that '*women should be non-violent*' terming it as '*political strategy of some opportunist group*'.

Thakuria, Rita Choudhury. *Legal Status of Women's Rights to Property, Right to Divorce etc. in Non-Tribal Societies of Assam*

Discusses the esteemed position of Indian women in the society during the Vedic period. Observes the deterioration in the status of Hindu women in the patriarchal form of society being influenced by the

Manusmriti. This article also traces the *'purdah'* system of Muslim Society. Highlights the contributions of Raja Rammohun Roy, and other social reformers like D N Tagore, Ishwar Chandra Vidyasagar, Swami Dayanand Saraswati. Focusses the involvement of women during the freedom struggle under the leadership of Mahatma Gandhi who championed for the restoration of the position of women in Indian society ordained in the constitution of independent India. The author also highlights some of the social reformers in Assam who advocated for the re-marriage of widows in the Assamese society.

Dealing with the issues of marriage and divorce the paper enumerates the rights envisaged in the Acts introduced to ensure security for women in all aspects of life from the claws of unscrupulous group of people in the society. Further analyses the inheritance rights and divorce under Muslim Law, adoption and maintenance of Children, Widow remarriage, Law–legalising Abortion, Immoral Traffic of Women, Laws for employment and Codification of Work for women. The author notes the ignorance of women of their own rights.

Pathak, Vijayalakshmi. *Women and Health Care*

This paper studies the general problems of women in health care. It stresses on health education for women and equal care to be given to baby girls without any prejudice. Advocates for special attention of health care for women as one of the basic human rights.

Mohanta, Paramanada. *Status of Women in Non-tribal Societies of Assam: Women and Health*

Discusses the discrimination against women in a

male-dominated society. Observes that in such society women do not enjoy fair health. It further analyses the state of health of women in India as reflected in various data on the sex-wise mortality rate, expectation of life, maternal and infant mortality, fertility and birth rate. Briefly highlights the status of women in non-tribal societies in Assam whose position in the society is a little higher compared to others in India. However, superstitions and taboos for girls and women pose a health hazard to women. Concludes that social attitudes towards women should be changed. Further suggests general awareness and education about health, pregnancy and related problems for precautionary measures against fatalities.

STATUS OF WOMEN IN BARAK VALLEY

Status of Women in Barak Valley: Organised by North Eastern Institute of Anthropological Research, Silchar, held at Karimganj on November 26-27, 1988. The Seminar was inaugurated by Dr. S B Nandi, Deputy Director, Anthropological Survey of India, Ministry of Human Resources Development, Government of India. In three academic sessions, chaired by Dr. K K Jha, Professor M N Kama and Dr. Shibani Roy respectively twenty research papers were presented on the occasion.

Bhattacharjee, Bimalendo. ***The Role of Barman Women in Barman Society***

This paper highlights the role of women in the Barman patriarchal society in education, religion, economic activity and marriage.

Bhattacharjee, Manjulika. ***Participation of Women in Freedom Movement in Karimganj***

Highlights the activities of Karimganj Mahila Sangha

during the period of 1930-1937. A list of women freedom fighters imprisoned during the Civil Disobedience Movement is also included and discussed in this paper.

Bhattacharjee, S. *Women Folk of the Fishermen Community in Chatta Town–An Overview*

Discusses the status of women in Chatta town with reference to their health, educational, social, economic standing in society.

Biswas, C K. *Status of Rongmei Women in Kagniluang Barak Valley*

Discusses the participation of women in decision-making in Rongmei society. Also observes their economic liberty determined by their status.

Choudhury, Aparajita. *Changing Role of Women in Barak Valley*

Studies the role of women in Barak. Analyses the position of women in the *'male dominated,' 'conservative male'* and *'traditional female'* societies. Further, gives a comparative study of the educated women in urban and rural areas of Barak Valley after the partition. Focusses on factors responsible for the changing role of women in the valley. Finally, advocates for equal rights to women as envisaged in the constitution.

Choudhury, Sujit. *A Female Rite of Barak Valley and its Social Significance*

Discusses the annual ceremonial celebration of the war-god being observed on the last day of the Bengalee month in Cachar. Further, the author throws more light on the association of the god with womenfolk.

Huda, Chabi. ***Status of Manipuri Muslim Women in Barak Valley***

Briefly gives the background of the Manipuri Muslim community living in the Barak Valley. Discusses the discrimination and suppression of women among the Manipuri Muslim society. Appeals for uplift of women for progress and prosperity of the state and the country.

Roy, Shibani. ***Contemporary Indian Women with Special References to Muslim Women***

Evaluates the status of women in contemporary Indian society. Raises some points on the importance of women in the society and the actual status of women within the family which gives a true picture of the position of women.

Roy, Shibani and S H M Rizvi. ***Power, Land and Women***

Investigates women's right to property and land. Power in decision-making is also discussed.

Soha, N. ***Status of Women: Some Theoretical Considerations***

Gives a theoretical study of the status of women referring to the works of various social scientists.

Sen (Das), M. ***Women Employment Today in India vis-a-vis Karimganj District***

Highlights the actual position of women in the family and society. Discusses their position in the labour market. Finally, suggests measures for the betterment of women.

STATUS OF WOMEN IN PLAINS TRIBAL SOCIETIES OF ASSAM: TRADITION AND CHANGE

Organized by the Department of Folklore Research, Gauhati University, January 15-20, 1989. Dr D P Baruah, Vice-Chancellor, Gauhati University inaugurated the seminar while Smti Indira Miri was the Chief Guest on the occasion. In the two academic sessions, 16 papers were presented during the seminar with Dr. Renu Devi and Dr. B M Das in the chair respectively.

Bordoloi, B M. ***Status of Plains Tribal in Assam: From the view point of Education***

This paper analyses the low literacy rate of the plains tribal women in Assam comprising of the Barmans of Cachar, Boro-Kacharis, Deoris, Hojai, Kacharis, Sonowals, Lanungs, Miris and the Rabhas. Further discusses the problems faced by women in getting education and provides suggestions for proper education for young girls to improve their position and status in the society.

Barooah, Jeuti. ***Women in Pati Rabha Society: An Appraisal in the context of Customary Laws and Practices***

The author presents her findings in a field study conducted in the Ranjuli area of the Goalpara district and parts of Greater Guwahati in Kamrup district. Based on her study, she highlights the customary laws relating to marriage covering the aspect of polygamy practice, widow and widow-remarriage, dissolution of marriage by way of divorce, divorce by mutual consent, divorce ceremony, maintenance, inheritance and succession. She discusses the status and position of women in the contemporary Pati Rabha society in the light of the study of a cross-section of Rabha womenfolk. Observes the process of change taking place in the society.

Brama, Binny Kumar. ***The Status of Woman in the Tribal Society: With Reference to the Bodo Society***

This paper discusses the status of Bodo women according to the yardstick that a woman plays in the family with regard to her economic, social, religious and political participation.

Brahma, Kameswar. ***The Status of Bodo Women in the Society: With Special Reference of Kokrajhar District***

Discusses the social and family structure of the Bodo society with special reference to the Kokrajhar District. It highlights the position of women, their economic, social and political participation in the society.

Saikia, Paban Ch. ***Status of Women in Deuri Society***

Outlining the economic, social, cultural, political and religious aspects of the Deuri society, the author observes the major contribution of womenfolk in the household and agricultural activities. However, their status is believed to be below the level of the menfolk due to the traditional outlook, socio-economic conditions, and belief and practices of the society.

Buragohain, Joga. ***The Status of Women in the Aitae Society: Past and Present***

This is a study based on material collection from magazines and journals, references from census reports and field study. The paper attempts to trace the history of the Aiton people, the smallest tribal community of Assam with only five thousand population. The author notes with interest the high position held by womenfolk which is reflected in their participation in family life and cultural, social, economic and political life.

Gohain, Amiya Khan. ***The Status of Tai-Phake Women in Assam: Condition and Change***

Traces the history of the Tai-Phake. Highlights their social and family structure. Analyses the status of the women in the society, discusses their role and position as reflected in the customary law code, folkstories, socio-religious beliefs and practices as well as in their economic contribution. Observes the impact of education on the improvement of the status of women in the modern society. It also emphasizes on the need of preservation of their culture and language.

Kagyung, Bhriguram. ***Status of Women in the Mishing Community of Assam***

In the light of the dictionary meaning of the word, '*tribe*', this paper makes an attempt to discuss a sub-tribe of Assam included in the constitution of India 1950 and in the subsequent amendments made in 1976, identified as Mishing community of Assam. It reviews the data of the India's Census Report of 1971, and illiteracy rate of both male and female in the Mishing society. The unique role of Mishing women in the society is also observed in this paper.

Majumdar, D N. ***Some Basic Points for Consideration regarding Status of Women Particularly among the Plain Tribal Societies of Assam***

The author analyses the concept of the word '*status*'.

Makes an attempt to argue about the bias evident in the works of some writers in defining the status of women in different societies. Further highlights some of the works of the female writers who attempt to present the actual position of women.

Mitra, Kalyan. ***Status of Women among the Sonowal Kachari Tribe of Assam***

Briefly discusses the important role that women play in the Sonowal Kachari tribe of Assam. Elaborates their role in the rites and ceremonies of the new-born child in the family and their place in the society. The system of marriage and family is also discussed in this paper. Also studies the changes taking place in the society after the adoption of Neo- Vaishnavism.

Gohain, B K. ***Status of Women in the Society of Matrilineal Lalungs of Assam***

Discusses the aspects of the matrilineal system being followed by the Lalungs of Assam. Analyses the position of women in the Lalung society as reflected in the system of inheritance and succession, their social and economic participation in the society.

Pegu, Indreswar. ***Status of Women in the Mishing Community***

Gives a brief historical background of the Adi people in Arunachal Pradesh. Discusses the historical background of the migration of the Mishing people to the plain areas of Upper Assam and their assimilation with the plains people therein. Their acculturation to Hindu religion is also dealt with. Highlights the status of the Mishing women in the light of their spiritual, social and economic participation in the society. The impact of education among the women is also discussed. Finally, observes the commendable contribution of the Mishing women to the progress and development of the society.

Rabha, Heramba K. *Status of Rabha Women: In a Plain Tribal Society of Assam*

Elaborates the duty of a Rabha woman ranging from the domestic chores to the running of the poultry and agricultural activities in the society. Analyses the training given to women from childhood till she reaches the age of maturity. Discusses the property right of a woman, her place in the laws, and her role as a mother. Also the participation of female members during the naming ceremony of the new-born baby, death ceremony when it occurs in the family, among relatives, neighbours and friends. Their actual participation in the social, economic and cultural activities is also highlighted. Finally, observes the different attitudes of educated women towards traditional jobs.

Taid, Tabu. *The Mishing Women: Rights and Responsibilities*

Attempts to analyse the position of the Mishing women within the family and the community. Observes her better position compared to any other woman in the conservative societies.

Sharma Thakur, G C. *Status of Plains Tribal Women with Special Reference to the Mishing Women as reflected in 'Oi Nitams': Proverbs and Legends*

This paper discusses the position of the Mishing women as reflected in the folksongs.

Saikia, P C. *Acculturation in the Mishing Society in Silapathar Town, Lakhimpur, Assam*

Gives the salient features of the Mishing society based on the field investigation among the Mishings in Silapathar town.

STATUS OF WOMEN IN TRIBAL SOCIETIES (KARBI AND DIMASA)

Seminar organized by Diphu College, Diphu, Karbi Anglong on February 5, 1989. Smt. Nirupam Hajjer inaugurated the seminar. In two academic sessions, eighteen papers were presented with Dr. P S Datta (ICSSR-NERC) and Dr. G C Sharma Thakur (TRI, Assam) in the chair respectively. The proceedings of the seminar have been brought out in a book from entitled, *The Tribal Women*, edited by B C. Bhuyan (New Delhi, Omsons Publications, 1993, 101p).

Thakur, G C. ***Social Status of the Karbi Women as reflected in the Socio-cultural Life and Legends of the Karbis***

This study is based on the secondary sources and observations during the author's visit to Karbi villages.

Borah, Ashwini Kumar. ***The Status of Women in Karbi Society: An Observation***

Gives a brief account of the Karbis of Assam and the status of women in that society. The discussion focuses on their position in the family and their economic, religious, political and educational status. Lastly, the author presents his observations on the changing trend of the status of women, based on his survey conducted at Ramsingh Rongpi village of Howraghat.

Phangcho, P C. ***Status of Women in Karbi Society***

Traces the position of women from the legends and myths in the Karbi society. While analysing the rights being enjoyed by women in the society, the author argues on their deprivation from property rights and their limitations in taking part in administrative, religious and political matters.

Tado, Terangpi. ***The Role of Karbi Women in Society: Past and Present***

Highlights the indispensable role of women, right from childhood in the family as well as in the society. Further discusses their position at different stages of their womanhood as *'the Okarjang', 'the Jirasong'* their participation in religious rites called *'Chu Jun'*, and the two types of marriage among the Karbi people. Expresses appreciation on the success of Karbi women folk in different professional employment in the present (Karbi society) scenario.

Rongpi Gogoi, Minakshi. ***The Status of Women in Karbi Society***

The present article attempts to discuss the status of the Karbi women with reference to the traditional social system of the society. Observes the embracement of change in the Karbi society towards improvement of the position of women.

Medhi, G C. ***Women: Their Training and Status in Karbi Society***

Discusses the status of women and their participation and activity at different stages in the society during their childhood, adolescence, marriage and family life.

Terang, Rong Bong. ***The Place of Women in the Karbi Society according to the Folk Tradition***

Analyses the position of women in the Karbi society as reflected in the traditional marriage ceremony and the *'Cho Juns Pooja'*.

Pandey, Udai Bhanu. ***Karbi Women and the Male-Psyche: A Mythological Interpretation***

In this paper, the author seeks to interpret the status of Karbi women based on the mythology, folktales and expressive symbols of the Karbi society.

Duarah, Dharmeswar. ***The Traditional Status of Women in the Dimasa Society***

This work attempts to highlight the patrilineal and matrilineal system features of the Dimasa society. It also highlights the division of labour among the Dimasa people which demarcates the responsibility of women and men. Further discusses the status of women as reflected in their responsibilities. Finally, advocates for the improvement of the position of the Dimasa women by giving them equal education as enjoyed by their counterparts.

Bhattacharjee, Tanmoy. ***The Dimasa Female Clans and Some Problems***

Reviews the works of various writers dealing with the clan system of the Dimasa society, focussing on the emergence of the Barman Society, the codification of Sangphu and Lulu and the primary and secondary affiliation of the double system in the Dimasa society.

Naiding, Anupama. ***Position of Dimasa Women in Traditional Society***

Discusses the clan system of the Dimasa people and the place of women in the society. The commendable participation of women in economic activities is dealt with in this paper. Expresses appreciation on the social and economic independence of women in the society compared to other women in Indian society.

Voices the need of change of attitude towards education and political participation of women for a better society.

Nunisa, Motilal. *Status of Women in Tribal Societies (Dimasas)*

Presents the historical background of the racial affinity among the Dimasas. Defines the term *'Dimasa'*. Elaborates the clan system of women called *'Julu'*, the activities and responsibilities of women at different stages of womanhood, their role in the family, society, their economic contribution, right to inheritance and finally the author invites discussion on the question of *'Gusug Thar'* in the Dimasa society.

Thaosen, J L. *Status of Women in Dimasa Society*

Briefly discusses the Dimasa society. Outlines the economic, social, cultural and political participation of the Dimasa women. Studies the status of women from the qualities which they uphold in the society.

Chetia, Jiban. *The Status of Women in Tribal Societies (Karbi and Dimasa)*

Comments on the high percentage of illiteracy rate among the Karbi women, the root cause responsible for their low status in the society. Briefly discusses their traditional dress and ornaments, marriage, economic and social status. Provides the list of both male and female *'Jiluks'*.

3

MANIPUR

STATUS OF WOMEN IN MANIPUR

The seminar on the *Status of Women in Manipur,* organized by the Department of History, Manipur University, was held at Imphal on September 23 & 24, 1988. It was inaugurated by Maharaj Kumari Binodini Devi, the most distinguished and reputed lady of Manipur. Seventeen papers were presented on the occasion.

Ray, A K. *Women Status – Some Basic Issues*

Attempts to discuss the problem of women status in the modern society from three different angles– juristic, normative and historic.

Arun Kumar, M C. *Sex Alienation in Meitei Society*

Defines the meaning of alienation. Discusses Meitei sex alienation on decision-making at family level and mate-selection at the time of marriage. Also discusses women in kin-groups and the dual image of woman in the society. Finally, observes the rapid change in the role of woman in a modernized and westernized Meitei society.

Irene, Salam. *Women of Imphal Today*

The work presents interviews of a cross-section of women of different communities in Imphal. Discusses the restrictions and constraints imposed on women in the joint family. The author also argues on the consciousness of working women and Women's Movement in Imphal. Advocates for extension of facilities to women to develop their potentialities in contributing to the society.

Devi, Ksh. Bimola. *A Study of the Urban Educated Elite Women in Manipur*

Gives an historical account of the contributions of women in building up the society in the state of Manipur from the early periods. Examines the attitude, manner and the role of the educated working women in the urban society and the factors that stand in the way of political development concerning women of Manipur. Highlights the role of women–socially, economically and politically. Analyses the opinions of the urban educated elite women on the shying away of women participation in politics.

Tikoo, Ratna. *The Socio-economic and Political Profile of Meitei Women*

Highlights the socio-economic and political profile of Meitei women in the light of past history, mythology, religious records and the present social setups.

Devi, M Shanti. *Education and the Changing Status of Women in Manipur*

Points out the vital economic contribution of women

in the Meitei society. Advocates for equal rights of women to education for the progress and development of the nation. Refers to the recommendations of University Education Commission, 1948 and Education Commission (1964-66). Discusses the condition of female education during pre-Independence period; the progress of female education after Independence and the changes in the status of women and the impact of western education among the women of Meitei society.

Sanchita Kumar. ***Non-Manipuri Women Living in the Manipur University Campus***

Underlines briefly the status of women of Manipur as viewed by non-Manipuri women and that of the non-Manipuri living in the Manipur University campus.

Sangkham, Gina. ***The Status of Women in the Moyon Society***

Discusses the position of Moyon women in the traditional and modern society.

Lalremsiem. ***Status of Women in Mizo Society: A Historical Study***

Discusses the position of women in the family, their right to property and their economic condition in the Mizo society.

Khaonam, Mahmoodah. ***The Status of Muslim Women in Manipur***

Discusses the position of Muslim women in Manipur in the present society. Focusses on their role in the system of marriage, divorce, polygamy, purdah, and their political participation and economic contribution to society.

Singh, M Bokul. ***The Tarao Women: Whether Changing to a Better Position?***

Presents two view points of the status of women in the tribal societies. Observes the high status of women in the matrilineal societies and the suppressive position of women in the patrilineal societies. Discusses the lineage pattern being followed in the Tarao patrilineal and patrilocal society, the system of inheritance, the actual treatment of the women, the practice of child marriage and social changes in the present society.

Gailangam, K. ***Status and Role of Rongmei Women***

Discusses the status and role of Rongmei women related to their participation in the family, society, religion, and politics, their involvement in the freedom movement, the question of property rights and their changing position in the modern society.

Varma, L B. ***Status of Women in Manipur***

Raises some of the questions through which the status of women in Manipur can be examined.

Lien, Z Z. ***The Hmar Women of Manipur***

Highlights the heroic participation of Hmar women in the battle of 'Nupi land'. Gives a brief outline of the socialization of women in the Hmar society from their childhood till they reach the age of maturity. The author also discusses the role and contributions of Hmar women in the society.

Lalremsang, Hmar. *Modern Education and the Status of Hmar Women*

Attempts to discuss the problems of Hmar women in Tripaimukh sub-division of Manipur–their economic backwardness, deprivation to rights of property and the evident sex bias. Suggests for improvement of the status of Hmar women in the modern society.

4

MEGHALAYA

THE EFFECTS OF THE MATRILINEAL SYSTEM ON PRESENT DAY KHASI SOCIETY

"The Effects of the Matrilineal System on Present Day Khasi Society," (Ka Jingiaphyllliew Jingmutlang Halor Kumno Ka Jingshimjait na ka Kmie ka ktah ia ka Imlang Sahlang jong ka Jaidbynriew) organised by Dr J. War, Reader, Department of English, NEHU held on 27 and 28th of May 1988 in Shillong. The Minister of Education, Meghalaya Mr J D Pohrmen was the Chief Guest on the occasion. In a two day seminar sixteen papers were presented on different aspects of the matrilineal system.

Lyngdoh, J Darningstone. *Ka Nongrim jong ka Jingshimjait na ki Kynthei hapdeng ki Khasi bad Pnar (the Basic Principle of the Matrilineal System in the Khasi-Pnar Society)*

Attempts to analyse some aspects on how matrilineal system was traditionally accepted by the Khasi-Pnar society. Discusses the role of a male member and the need for the system to adopt and be relevant to the changes in the present society. Alternative structure is also advocated.

Laitphlang, W R. ***Katto katne ki mat halor ka phang Kumno ka jingshimjait na ka kmie ka ktah ia ka imlang sahlang (Some Points on the Effects of Matrilineal System in the Society)***

Briefly discusses the concept of matrilineal system. Attempts to analyse the traditional culture of the Khasis and their democratic principle. Discusses the role of men and women in the society. The role of the youngest daughter as the custodian of the ancestral property is highlighted.

Rapthap, Krieshon. ***Katto katne ka jingktah ka rukom jingshimjait na ka kmie ia ka jaidbynbriew (Some of the Effects of the Matrilineal Society)***

Discusses the traditional concept of the matrilineal system. Analyses the present social changes in the society. The impact of inter-marriage in the society is also outlined for discussion.

Shadap, R. ***Ka jingshimjait hapdeng ki Khasi (The Matrilineal System in the Khasi Society)***

Attempts to analyse the changing situation in the Khasi society. The position of the father both in traditional and modern concept is discussed at length. Inter-marriage among the Khasis and different aspects of property inheritance both movable and immovable, in the context of women, discrimination of the male members, misuse of the ancestral property by the custodian, and self-acquired property are also analysed. The importance of education for the children in the modern context which is considered more valuable property is also asserted.

Passah, P M. ***Ka jingioh pateng ha ki kynthei ka ktah ia ka khih ka kamai ki shynrang (The matrilineal System of Inheritance, Its Effects on the Economic Activities of Males and Self-acquired Property of Male Members)***

Discusses some of the drawbacks of the system of inheritance in the Khasi society. Attempts to analyse opinions expressed by some personalities and social organisations through different media (newspapers, leaflets, constitutions etc.) Formation of some social movements for reformation and modification of the system is also discussed by the author.

Ngap Kynta, H B. ***Ka imlang sahlang bad ka trei ka ktah ha ka Ri ki Laiphew Syiem (Society and Private Enterprise in the Land of the Thirty Chiefs)***

Traces the involvement of the Khasi people in international trade about 200 years ago. The encroachment of the external forces since the time of British till date that transformed the economic culture of the Khasis is dealt briefly. The role of both men and women in sharing economic responsibility is also discussed. Lastly, the author asserts the capability and efficiency of the Khasi people in every field if opportunity were opened to them.

Pde, L H. ***Ka Jingshimjait na ka Kmie (The Matrilineal System)***

Asserts the unique system of the Khasi society, where man is the uncle in his clan, a father and head of the family to his children, and where a woman is the mother and grandmother to her children and grand children respectively. The pattern of inheritance and self-acquired property is discussed. The esteemed position of the youngest daughter as the custodian of the ancestral property, the keeper of the religion, in whose hearth all the religious ceremonies are being performed, the bearer of the expenditure for all ceremonial rites at time of distress of her brothers and sisters is dealt in detail.

Umdor, M B. ***Kumno ka jingshimjait na ka kmie ka ktah ia ka imlang sahlang jong ka jaidbynriew (The Effects of Matrilineal System in the Khasi Society)***

Deals with the social aspect and upbringing of the children in the Khasi society. Stresses on the responsibility of the parents in guiding and protecting the children from the external forces of social change, social evils and the influence of materialistic attitude in today's life.

Warjri, K M. ***Kajingiadei ki kmie ki kpa bad ki khun bad kumno ka ktah ia ka education kajong ki khun shynrang bad kynthei ha ka jaidbynriew (The Relationship between parents and Children and how it affects the Education of the Children)***

Gives a brief background of matrilineal system being followed by different societies other than the Khasi people of Meghalaya. Further, analyses the system of upbringing of the children in the Khasi society. The author also presents his research findings on parent- child relationship with reference to love and affection, security, status and responsibility, education, achievement and motivation of both sons and daughters. Finally, observes the higher rate of girls coming-up particularly in educational achievement as compared to boys in the Khasi matrilineal society.

Nongkynrih, A Kyrham. ***The Upbringing of Children in a Matrilineal Society (Ka jingpynheh pynsan ia ki khun ha ki ing Khasi haba shimjait na ka kmie)***

Describes the structural organisation of the society. Discusses the system of upbringing of children in the matrilineal society based on the survey reports conducted in St Mary's College and St Anthony's College.

Khonglah, C. ***How does the Matrilineal System affect Society? (Kumno ka jingshimjait na ka kmie ka ktah ia ka imlang sahlang)***

Gives a critical analysis of some of the forces responsible for the misinterpretation of the unique system of the matrilineal society.

Lyngdoh, M P R. ***The Matrilineal System and Politics (Kajingshimjait na ka kmie bad ka kam sain hima sima- ki kynthei haka kam sa in hima sima)***

Examines the traditional concept of the matrilineal System in the Khasi society. Further analyses the position of women in the early period and present situation. Their political participation is discussed highlighting the opinions and role of some noted writers, public leaders and prominent figures in the field. Advocates for the active participation of women in politics.

War, Juanita. ***The Matrilineal System and Social Change in the Khasi Society***

Outlines the main factors responsible for the present social change in the Khasi society.

Syiem, I M. ***Some Observations in the Problem of Change in Khasi Matrilineal System***

Attempts to highlight some of the important areas of change within the Khasi matrilineal system. The author focusses on aspects of the Khasi matriliny and structural adjustment; religion and change; role of men; decision-making; and social interaction of maternal uncle with his maternal kins. Observes some of the evidence of change in inter-personal relationships in the society especially in family and kinship relationships.

Pariat, Ellerene Cunville. ***How the Matrilineal System Affects the Khasi Society?***

Attempts to examine some of the factors affecting the matrilineal system in the Khasi society.

Basaiawmoit, Enid Richmond. ***Attitudes towards the Matrilineal System***

Observes the dramatic changes in the Khasi society under the influences of education, religion, technology, politics etc. Reports the findings of her study conducted among the sample of 500 Khasi working women in Shillong.

STATUS OF WOMEN IN TRIBAL CULTURE OF MEGHALAYA

Seminar organized by the Centre for Literacy and Cultural Studies, NEHU, held on 13-14 July, 1988. The papers presented during the seminar have been brought out in a book form, entitled *Women in Meghalaya*, by Soumen Sen (Ed). (New Delhi, Omsons, 1997).

The present volume contains seven chapters including the introduction and reports of the Editor and

Rappouteur, Shri Abhijit Choudhury. The papers provide informations and insider's views on the status and role of women in the matrilineal societal context of Khasi-Jaintia and Garo Hills of Meghalaya both in the traditional setup and in the changing scenario.

War, Juanita. ***Status of Women in Traditional Khasi Culture***

Analyses the role of women in general and traces the vital role of Khasi women in the society covering family organisation, economic, political and administrative fields, social and cultural participation of women. Highlights the position of the youngest daughter as the custodian of family property under the guardianship of the *'durbar'* of uncles and brothers i.e. maternal males. Focusses on the present position of women in the society particularly on the impact of education as one of the factors responsible for social change.

Syiem, I M. ***Women in Khasi Society***

Raises few questions on equal rights for women and refers to Women's Liberation Movements. Briefly noted the distinctively better position and status of Khasi women as compared with other women in the patrilineal society. Examines the traditional Khasi society and the role of maternal uncles, brothers, fathers, women and the youngest daughter in different aspects of life. Analyses the assertion of women in various fields at present. Points out the limited participation of Khasi women in politics in the process of legislation both at the District Council and State Legislative Assembly. Observes the reluctance among the Christian women to taking a leading role in the Churches.

Passah, P M. ***Status of Women in the Jaintia Culture***

Examines the role of women in Jaintia society. Traces their traditional role in the family, in religious matters, economic activities, social and political spheres. Highlights the impact of education and Christianity on women in today's life. Concludes with a plea for equal rights to property under the unique matrilineal system of the Jaintia society to be also extended to men.

Gassah, L. ***Status of Women in Jaintia Hills***

Refers to some studies conducted both by local and non-local scholars on the question of the status of men and women, law of inheritance, descent, succession and the issue of matrilineal system in general. Discusses the esteem and respect given to women right from birth, the responsibility entrusted to them from childhood focussing on their role in family and social life including religious matters, their economic involvement and participation in and outside their homes. Observes the restrictions imposed on women from participating in decision-making in the traditional political institutions.

Marak Caroline R. ***Status of Women in the Garo Culture***

Discusses the concept and position of women in the traditional Garo society. Asserts the capability of the Garo women to participate in the present society on account of the advent of education and Christianity. These two factors are responsible in raising and improving the status and role of Garo women in the present Garo society.

WOMEN, PEACE AND DEVELOPMENT WITH SPECIAL REFERENCE TO MEGHALAYA

Organised by the Indian Council of Social Science Research of the North Eastern Regional Centre, Shillong held on 21st October, 2000. Professor Imdad Hussain, Hony. Director inaugurated the seminar in a function chaired by Professor L.S. Gassah. Eight papers were presented on the occasion.

Rapthap, H M. *Women and Peace*

In his paper, H M Rapthap speaks of *'Peace'* associated with tranquility, quietness, silence, freedom from war, freedom from civil disorder, freedom from strife or any kind of disorder. But with the growing menace in the society today, particularly the mushrooming of the militants in the region he points out the irrelevance of the word *'Peace'* in today's society. Observing the present situation of violence and strife, he reminds us of our bounded duty as citizens including children to make the world a place conducive to live in. He expresses his optimism and hope that women in their various roles, as well as women's organizations will be committed to initiate positive social changes and bring about peace and harmony in society. He cites the example of the Mother's Union, Garo Hills in their role of negotiating for peace with violent militant youth groups. Appreciating the leadership of women, he stressed the need for giving due recognition to women in their contribution to the society.

Mawlong, M R. *Empowering of Women – Social, Economic and Political*

This paper briefly discusses the role of Khasi-Jaintia and Garo women of the matrilineal societies of

Meghalaya. It highlights the marginalization of women in decision-making in the traditional bodies as well as in political spheres in spite of enjoying electoral politics. Speaking of empowerment of women, the author shares the same views with other papers in recognizing the need for gender equality in the society.

Lyngdoh, M P R. *Women and Peace in the North East*

As violence begets violence, therefore, 'shun the path of *violence*' is the slogan of this paper. To initiate the discussion, quoting from Mahatma Gandhi, the Father of the Nation, *'Peace is the only weapon that can bring prosperity and all round development in any of the world'*, Lyngdoh analyses the contributions of the world leaders and other great personalities of the world. In her observation over the absence of *'Peace'* in the present society, she strongly believes that, 'Peace is the need of the hour in the whole world, and women have a great role to play in the mission of peace making. With their endurance, sacrifice and moral courage, there is nothing they cannot do for mankind. Elaborating further on the role of women in general, she states that women can play a very important and significant role in all walks of life as they do not get tired of work mentally, physically, spiritually for the welfare and development of the society. From the development point of women, she defines development as a socio-economic and political process which requires an equal active participation of both men and women. To have a people-oriented development, she stresses on the elimination of the words, discrimination, deprivation, violence, suffering from our mind-set. Driving home the deliberation, she refers to the social and economic independence of women being free from many of the social restraints of the larger Indian society, of course, keeping in mind the prevalence of other social problems, that women in Meghalaya are facing in the society. To bring peace in the society, she urges upon the government to initiate steps to promote peace suggesting a people-oriented development, besides making self-retrospection particularly women to keep their hearths and home violence-free. She also calls upon women organizations to work together in order to bring peace and progress, specially the women workers at the grassroot levels. In conclusion, she lauds the negotiating role played by the Garo Mother's Union and the Naga Mother's Association in bringing peace and harmony in the region.

Ranee, F. ***Religion as a Catapult for Social Change and the Role of Women in Peace Building***

This paper discusses the significant role played by religion in the field of development and progress. Examining the power of religion in bringing about social change, the author raises the question of the type of change in the present society. She expresses her opinion for preservation of traditional values. She also sees the need of identification of relevant areas that require change in the society. In doing so, we should seek guidance from 'our spiritual consciousness' and 'our religious principles', she added. Referring to 'Fear of God and Love of Neighbour', she believes in spiritual values of Swami Vivekananda, that of *Purity, Patience* and *Perseverance,* the three essentials to success, and above all, *Love'*. She further emphasizes on the need to practice these virtues in our everyday lives and to also change our attitude towards religion and our lukewarm approach to Education, Economics,

Administration, Family Life, Inter-community relationship and Politics. A positive outlook is needed so that corruption, ethnic conflicts and communal disharmony, which are the enemies of our social being, can be uprooted to make way for all-round progress. She also cautioned of the fanaticism and fundamentalism which lead to intolerance resulting in unrest and violence in the society today. Today she said, there is a clarion call to all right thinking people to fight these unwanted elements and to prevent them from contaminating our societies. She felt that the world which is in need of *'liberation'* from these anti-social forces look up to women to lend a helping hand and rise up to this challenge. She invites them to come forward as the ardent and devout practitioners of religious faith and turn their homes into little churches and temples for the development and progress within their families and society and to enable them to strive for *'Peace'*.

Syiem, I M. *Women, Religion and Change*

This paper is divided into four parts. The first part deals briefly with the definition of women, religion and change. In the second part it discusses the historical background of the issues under reference. The third part highlights the impact of women's movement in the society. The last part reflects some of the author's observations on women and change in Northeast through religion.

Analysing the impact of women's movement, Syiem remarks on the emergence and increasing support of the movement and of its focus on women's rights, and voicing of their grievances. She further maintains that the women's movement which highlights women's perspectives in the general affairs of life has gained momentum despite cultural, religious and social resistance. The more women were abused, exploited their cause were taken up, exposed, supported and generated fuel to the movement.

Discussing on the concept of women, religion and change, Syiem found it to be more simpler to define such abstract concepts as religion and change than to define today's concept of women. In her opinion, it is less difficult to define women within the traditional context and specific historical time frames. According to her, traditionally, women accepted their limited roles in religious activities, economic life and the larger social life. Further, states that the individual status of women depends on the family status and personal liberty confined within the socially accepted norms of behaviour with a few exceptions. Observing the situation of women in general she found that the status of women was inferior in spite of the attempt of some social and religious reformers to uplift and improve women's condition as there was a lack of initiative from women themselves to bring about change.

Nongkynrih, A K. *Gender and Development: Rural Reality in Meghalaya*

Seeking to understand the word *'Gender'* an issue of debate resulting from the interpretations of various intellectual traditions, the author presents a theory of feminism for the purpose of analyzing the study carried out in Khatar Shnong, a rural village within the state of Meghalaya. Based on the data collected, Nongkynrih analyses the issues of women's development in the Khasi matrilineal society.

Chhakchhuak, Linda. *Media as an Instrument of Peace and Development*

Discusses briefly the role of the media in

disseminating information to the masses. This paper also expresses its appreciation of the initiative taken by the local newspaper particularly 'Mawphor' in organizing an essay competition on *"Future of the Khasi Society in the 21st Century"*, giving space to the young participants to express their great apprehension for the future of the Khasi society.

Nongbri, C & Dkhar, R. *Education as an Agent of Peace and Development – Role of Women in Society with Special Reference to Meghalaya*

This paper identifies some of the issues causing violation of peace in the society. The writers emphasize the need for the all-round development of people and society and suggest education as the need of the hour. In a society where women are educated there is an advantage. Educated women can take the initiative of setting up organizations for the purpose of bringing peace and development in the society. Finally, this paper highlights the activities of women organizations in Meghalaya in bringing peace and harmony in the state.

5

MIZORAM

STATUS OF WOMEN IN TRIBAL SOCIETIES OF MIZORAM

Status of Women in Tribal Societies of Mizoram, held at Aizawl on 29th July 1988 organised by Pachhunga University College. The seminar was well represented by various women organizations, government officials, prominent citizens, the college teaching community, and retired and noted personalities of Aizawl.

Sangkima. ***Women in the Traditional Mizo Society, Their Place in the Family and Society***

Gives a brief historical background of the Mizo society. Analyses the position of women in Mizo society in the family and in the society in general. Finally, observes the due recognition given to women.

Lalbiaktluanga. ***Mizo Women through History***

Analyses the position of Mizo women during the early period to the present scenario. Focusses their participation in the family, in politics, in economic life and their response to the process of Christianity, to education and social change.

Gohain, Prafulla. ***The Role of Women in Economic Development of Mizoram***

Studies the economic contribution of women in Mizoram. Observes their participation in domestic chores, cultivation, petty business and the negligible number of women working in government services and teaching profession as reflected in census Reports and Statistical Handbook.

Sarma, Surendranath. ***Status of Women in the Assamese Society***

Studies the status of Assamese women with reference to marriage and education as the two important factors determining the position of women.

Laltlani, P C. ***Mizo Women and the Church***

Highlights the role of Mizo women in Church activities right from the advent of Christianity in Mizoram.

Liandingi, P. ***Mizo Women and Social Control: Role of Women Organisation in maintaining Social Stability, Family Harmony and Movements against Social Problems***

Briefly gives the origin of the Mizo people. Discusses the position of women before the abolition of the chieftainship in Mizoram. Refers to the participation of women in decision-making in the village and District Councils, as well as at the state level political administration. Analyses the literacy rate of females in Mizoram and the percentage of women in government services in different districts and also their role in economic participation in the fields other than government jobs. Highlights the changes taken place in the position of women after embracement of Christianity by the Mizo people. Asserts the initiative taken by the Mizoram State Social Welfare Advisory Board, in motivating various women welfare organisations to exert and uplift womenfolk and also to deal with social evils in the society.

Hluna, J V. ***Education and Change – Impact on Mizo Women***

Discusses the impact of Christian missionaries on women education in Mizo society as a major factor responsible for the change in the negative attitude towards uplift of women.

Nath, K P. ***Education and Change with the Women in the Mizo Society***

The author gives a brief background of the conservative Mizo society in the past. Discusses the discrimination of education towards women. Observes the impact of education on Mizo women, who today are faring as well as that of their male counterpart in all spheres. A summary of the role of Mizo Hmeichhe lnsuihkhawm Pawl, a women's non-religious and non-political organisation is also highlighted.

6

NAGALAND

THE STATUS OF WOMEN IN NAGA SOCIETIES

"The Status of Women in Naga Societies", organized by the Naga Students' Union, Shillong on November 23, 1988 was held at Nagaland House, Shillong. Professor M.N. Karna, Department of Sociology, NEHU was the Chief Guest on the occasion, while Professor J.B. Bhattacharjee, Department of History, NEHU, chaired the first business session, while Professor Kama conducted the second session.

The proceedings of the seminar is available in a printed form, entitled, *Women in Naga Society*, edited by Lucy Zehol, with an addition of some articles and an introduction by the Editor as Chapter 1. Naga society is comprised of different tribes and sub-tribes spread over Nagaland, Manipur, Assam and Arunachal Pradesh with their own local dialects. Interestingly, the communication among the different tribes is Nagamese and English. The papers included in the volume covered 12 tribes of the Naga society and an abstract of each is given below accordingly.

Warjri, K M. ***Educational and Social Problems faced by Women***

Discusses the discrimination, exploitation and suppression of Asian women in education, property rights, health care, religion, and the use of new technology to prevent the birth of female child. Refers to laws passed by various Asian countries to improve the status of women and to the UN Declaration of the Rights of the Child.

Mao, John. ***Status of Women in Naga Society***

Gives the definition of the term *'status'* referring to the works of various scholars. Discusses the views on the position of women during the Vedic period, before and after Independence, mobilization of women's participation during the freedom movement launched by Mahatma Gandhi as part of reforming the status of Indian women and emancipation through education, status of women in tribal society of North-East India, demographic profile of the tribal population, modern tribal women in the political sphere and education of tribal women. Analyses the position of women economically, socially, politically, academically and culturally.

Thomas, Lucy. ***The Tangkhul Women Today***

Raises the question of *'status of women'* in the society. Discusses the social independence and economic participation of women in the patrilineal society of the Tangkhul people in Manipur. The system of inheritance according to the Tangkhul customary law is also highlighted. The position of Tangkhul women in the traditional society is also dealt with. Outlines the factors responsible for social change in the

Tangkhul society. Poses some questions on the social disturbances affecting the progress of education among the Tangkhul girls.

Tungoe, Mhatung. ***Status of Women in the Lotha Society***

Traces the origin of the Lotha society. Focusses the position of women both in the traditional and modernized society. Stresses on the need for women to exert themselves in order to receive recognition in the society.

Mao, Xavier. ***The Status of Women in Mao Society***

Discusses the theoretical and conceptual issues relating to the status of women, their actual role in the Mao community. This paper focusses on birth ceremonies, marriage and illegitimate children in the Mao community. Observes the urgency of change to improve the position of women.

Newmai, Hunibou. ***The Status of Women in Zeliangrong Naga Society***

Analyses the historical background of the three sub-tribes of Zeliangrong Nagas, the Zemei, Liangmai and Rongmei spread in Assam, Nagaland and Manipur. Discusses the status of women in the patriarchal system, the pattern being followed by the Zeliangrong Nagas, the practice of bride-price and the impact of Christianity and western education in the society. Raises questions on the deprivation and discrimination of women. Advocates for equal rights to women and to give due recognition for their contributions in the family and in the society.

Newmai, Hunibou. ***The Status of Women in Zeliangrong Naga Society***

Presents a historical background of the Zeliangrong

society, which separated after a conflict over a chieftainship of the three brothers later known as Zemei, Liangmei and Rongmei inhabiting Assam, Nagaland and Manipur respectively speaking different dialects; but having a similar tradition, customary laws, traditional customs, folksongs, folkdances, folktales and other cultural similarities. While discussing the status of women in the Zeliangrong society, Newmai maintains the inequality towards women in this patriarchal society. As the physically weaker section, women are being protected, however, they are being deprived of the share of the ancestral property, and there is unequal treatment from their own parents. They are also debarred from participation in any decision-making processes. The practice of bride price is also discussed in this paper. A consolation to women in the society is that they play an important role in the domestic affairs, as stated by the writer. Some changes in their status is also noted with the advent of Christianity and western education, as they are allowed to attend public meetings and give speeches. However, there is still parents' preference to boys for the male child. In conclusion, the author advocates for a recognition of the contribution of women and for them to be treated equally as human beings, the creation of the same God.

Zhimoni, Salomi, *The Status of Women in Sema Society*

Examines the traditional and modern aspects of the Sema people focussing on the role of women in the society.

Kelhou, *Women in Angami Society*

This paper briefly presents the facets and status of Angami women in the traditional and the modern society. The presentation focuses on the factors relating to economic, social and religious matters. It further examines the status and role of women as wife, daughter, sister and mother; on women organizations with special reference to Angami Women Organization, Kewhimie Zhovipgiiko Krotho; the role of the church in relation to women welfare and status of women in general. It also discusses the spread of education among women, the population ratio of male-female in the urban and rural areas. Finally, highlights some illustrious women in the Angami society.

Zehol, Kevekha and Zehol. Lucy, *Women in the Chakhesang (Chokri and Khezha) Society*

In this chapter, the authors made an attempt to explore the historical background of the Chakhesang referring to the earlier writer, Hutton who defined this tribe under reference as Eastern Angamis comprising of Chokri, Khezha and the Sangtam. However, the latter tribe broke away from this common identity and maintain their own separate identity till date. In the light of their different traditional background, this study examines the status of women in the Khezha and Chokri societies discussing the aspects of marriage, observation of moral values, the practice of maintaining of girl's and boy's dormitory, social gatherings and entertainment on special feast days. The other areas included are women's economic position, inheritance, shared property in case of divorce, participation of women in festival, myths about women, Ngei pi-O or the spirit associated with wealth and riches, their role as the Mawopi or village priestess and participation of women in the village assembly. However, the paper underlined the changes taken place in the present social transformation in the Naga society and the change among the women in the Chakhesang society in particular.

Zehol, Kevekha and Zehol, Lucy. *Konyak Women*

Attempts an exploratory study of women amongst the Konyak tribe. Based on this study, this chapter analyses the role and status of Konyak women in the society underlining some of the restrictions and taboos imposed on women. It also highlights the place of women in festivals, rituals and religious ceremonies. It also touches on the practice of arranged marriage in the society, separation and divorce. The economic contribution of women besides domestic chores dominates the deliberation in this study. The role played by the Konyak women as mediator on occasion of urgency to pacify the warring villages is drawn in the course of analysis reflecting the status of women in the society. With the advent of Christianity and western education women in the Konyak society welcome the modifications, improvement especially for the development of women. A women welfare organization which has also been rendering a great service in attempting to eradicate social evils in the society is also highlighted briefly in the study.

Kath, Shiloh. *Women in the Rengma Society*

Briefly discusses the role of women in the Rengma society with reference to their position in the traditional society, their participation in the management of property and inheritance, and equal wages among men and women in occupation. Other aspects included for discussions are position of women in case of divorce, their participation in social and religious matters, women in the changing society, their role as women welfare organization and in the church.

Aier, Anungla. *Women in Ao Society*

In her paper, Aier asserts of the better position being enjoyed by the Ao women compared to any other women in tribal societies. The present work attempts to project an objective understanding of the status of women in Ao Naga society. In the light of this objective, the position of Ao women is discussed in this paper, highlighting the issues related to economic, social, religious, political and village administration and women's participation in the society. Finally, highlights the role of western education and Christianity among the women in the Ao society.

7

TRIPURA

STATUS OF WOMEN IN THE SOCIETIES OF TRIPURA

Status of Women in the Societies of Tripura, organised by the Tripura University on January 14, 1989 held in the Council Room of the University. Professor J.B. Ganguly, Vice-Chancellor of the Tripura University gave an inaugural address on the occasion while Dr M. Das Gupta introduced the theme. Six papers were presented in three business sessions. Papers presented on the occasion including two additional papers have been brought out in a book form, entitled *Status of Women in Tripura,* edited by Malabika Das Gupta. (New Delhi, Vikas Publishing House, 1993, p. 79). This volume contains eight chapters.

Chakravarty, Manik. ***Customary Laws and the Status of Tribal Women in Tripura***

Presents a brief survey of some customary laws of tribal women of Tripura. This work also attempts to explore the legal ways by which the status of women can be raised from their deplorable conditions. Discusses the vital role of women in the family, religion, and their succession to ancestral property.

Pleads for modification of the customary laws to protect women from suppression and exploitation. Advocates for the changing attitudes of the society towards women to uplift their position.

Chaudhuri, Dipak Kumar. ***The Sati in Tribal Societies of Tripura***

Notes the practice of Sati among the Jamatias of Tripura during the 19th century referring to some of the official documents as evidence. *'Sati'* was practiced by the tribal people as part of their religious and cultural custom.

Chakravarti, Tapati. ***Notes on Tribal Female Work Participation in Tripura: Some Aspects***

Analyses the work participation of tribal women in Tripura taking the data from different census Reports of 1960-1981. Highlights the low literacy rate of females in the tribal society, particularly among the Riang people. Discrimination of various facilities to women is also discussed. Pleads for the improvement of the status of women through literacy programmes, training of professional and technical skills among them.

Choudhury, Pratap. ***Status of Women in the Tribal Societies of Tripura***

Discusses the status of women in Kuki, Chakma, Halam, Reang, Jamatia, Kaipong, Moghs, Garos, and Uchuis societies of Tripura referring to the works of various noted writers.

Das Gupta, Malabika. ***Bride-price and the Status of Riang Women in Tripura***

Discusses the practice of marriage by service among

the Riang people of Tripura living in remote areas. Highlights the findings from the survey report conducted in the village of Narayanbari. The indispensable economic contribution of women in the Riang society is also discussed. Analyses the status of women by using demographic and social indicators for the purpose of the study. Observes limited activity of various social movements to create awareness and educate this particular backward place about various social evils.

Debnath, Chhanda and Sircar, Bithi. ***Riang Mothers at Risk: A Nutritional Case-study on Reang Women of North Tripura***

Attempts to identify the causes of maternal ill-health in the Riang society focussing on their nutritional diets. Suggests for launching special nutritional programmes and other developmental programmes to combat malnutrition among Riang women and their future generation.

Bhattacharjee, P R. ***Adding a Gender Dimension to Tribal Studies***

This paper seeks to study the concept of gender from the point of view of the problems and prospects relating to women which a society has within its own system. In this context, the author maintains the existence of gender inequality in every tribe which is no different in Tripura society. Women's studies should not be guided by emotions or prejudice but it needs to be determined by different factors which will give a more complete picture of women's status in any tribe.

Ganguly, J B. ***The Status of Tribal Women in the Post- Jhuming Stage of Tribal Economy in Tripura (A case study of Herma village in West Tripura District)***

Based on a visit for preparing a development plan for the village of Herma, the author observes the economic contribution of women, the social and economic independence of women despite their being inferior to men. However, the status and position of women have improved in the present society. During his visit, he saw the hard working, women participating in different productive activities to meet the needs of their family members. This made him to make a comment on the vital role of women which keeps the village economy going. Being impressed with their pragmatic, hardworking and progressive outlook, he states that no village development plan can be prepared and implemented without the active involvement of the women of the village.

WOMEN AND EDUCATION

Seminar on *"Women Education: Its Role on Social Change,"* organised by Pub-Kamrup College on 3rd December 1993. Shri Syed Maniruddin Ahmed gave an inaugural address while the keynote address was given by Dr Renu Das on the occasion.

Deka, Hem Chandra. ***Women Education: Its Role on Social Change***

Discusses social change on the basis of modification of *'status'* and *'role'* brought about by the factors such as technology, industry, economy and religion. The author underlines the changes brought about (a) political situation, (b) economic growth, (c) scientific and technological development as a result of education, and (d) philosophical thinking and the consciousness of educated women about their own capabilities which brought about changes in some orthodox views in the society. Notes the landmarks in the history of the growth and development of education in Assam after the *Treaty of Yandaboo,* the contribution of missionaries towards women education and its role on social change.

Deka, Birendra. ***Women Education: Its Role on Social Change***

Gives a historical background of education of women in India. Briefly highlights the *Report of Education Commissions* and *Committees* relating to women education. Analyses the role of women on social change and women and their status in the society. Stresses on women education for progress and prosperity.

Saikia, Kula. ***Women Education and Social Changes: Some Issues***

Raises some basic issues pertinent to women education and social changes. Emphasises on the need for political education among women and also urges for creation of congenial environment in developing the potentials of women.

Kalita, Uma Kanta. ***Woman Education: Its Role on Social Change***

Views women's participation as an indisputable factor towards development and progress in the society. Discusses the issue of woman's compulsory academic and technical education as enunciated by

Gandhiji, the programme launched in the 1st Five Year Plan. Highlights the role being played by the Industries Department (Cottage Industries) in Technical Education for women in Assam and many other educational institutions.

Goswamee, Gayatree. ***Social Transformation through Women's Education***

Maintains the key role of education in the process of modification of the life-style of the people in the society. Makes an analytical study of the issues of social transformation related to women's education, social injustice and women's education, political injustice, population explosion and women's education, literacy of the people, and action programme for the future. Reiterates the call of Mahatma Gandhi for educating the masses.

Dev Chaudhury, Balen. Science Education: Some Problems Confronted Women

Discusses the social and gender constraints faced by women in pursuing science education or higher education, the problems being posed by the society or by their biological limitations.

Daam, Debajani. ***Women Education: Its Role on Social Change***

Examines the relationship between education and social change. Briefly discusses women and the right to education in the democratic system of a country like India. Poses some questions relating to policy making and social change for discussion.

WOMEN AND URBANISATION

Seminar on *Urbanisation, Status of Women and Structural Adjustment in the North East,* organised by Women's College, Shillong held on December 2, 1995. Five papers were presented on the occasion.

Bhattacharjee, Sukalpa. ***An Alternative Women's Paradigm for Structural Adjustment: Agenda of Cultural Protest in the North East***

This paper attempts to raise the issue of women's 'representation' in the third world countries where women are playing an indispensable role. Yet the author notes the fact that women are being pushed to the periphery of participating in decision-making particularly the women of North East India. On the other hand, the author views the women of North East, the tribal societies in particular to have traditionally enjoyed a respectable position particularly in the tribal societies, however, expressed shock over the erosion of their position which they seem to have lost with the advent of the capitalist economy. The impact of urbanization on women is also discussed. Speculating on the emergence of the global market, she cautions womenfolk of North-East on any kind of exploitation in the name of economy. She also formulates some hypothesis for women how to safeguard the resources of this region from any threat resulting from 'globalisation.'

Biswas, Prasenjit. ***Debate between Matriliny and Patriliny in Khasi Society: Paradox(es) of Structural Adjustment***

This paper reflects a debate between matriliny and patriliny in the Khasi society. The author mainly highlights the opinions of the noted scholars, Tiplut Nongbri as reflected in the article entitled, '*Tribal*

Women and the Family in the Context of Meghalaya', presented in the seminar on *Changing Aspects of Family in Meghalaya* and also of the view of B. Pakem, in his foreword, *A Few Words About the Book* in *The Khasis and their Matrilineal System* by Pynshai Bor Syiemlieh. The author also analysed the implication of the structural adjustment programme of the global economy in the Khasi society if change comes as advocated.

Lall, Isabella. *Urbanization and Its Impact on the Mizo Women in Shillong*

Presents a case study of the Mizo people who migrated and settled in Shillong since 1960s focussing on the impact of urbanization on Mizo women of Shillong, one of the cities in North East. Observes the changes taking place in Mizo family, in terms of sharing the responsibility by the parents in bringing-up the children and maintenance of the family affairs, and in marriage and divorce. Highlights the supportive role of women in the church. Analyses the activities of the Mizo Welfare Society of Shillong.

Gogoi, Nitul Kumar. *The Second Shift*

Examines the problems faced by a modem Assamese family where both husband and wife are working to meet the increasing needs of the present day life. Further discusses the ideology of gender equality as a strategy in resolving the conflict.

WOMEN AND DEVELOPMENT

Women's Development: Problems and Prospects. organised by Department of Public Administration, NEHU, Mizoram Campus, Aizawl. Shri P R Kyndiah, Governor of Mizoram inaugurated the seminar while Shri L B Thanga, IAS (Retd) presided over the function.

Professor R Lalthantluanga, Pro-Vice Chancellor, NEHU gave a valedictory address and Shri P. Lalrihthanga, IAS (Retd) presided over the valedictory session.

Thanga, L B. *Women's Development: Problems and Prospects*

Attempts to study the harassment and ill-treatment of women in India particularly in societies other than the backward and tribal communities. Observes that women in the tribal societies of North East have a better position. Stresses on the need to recognise the important role played by women in cultural, social and economic development. Raises the question of equality between men and women. Further, calls for a change in traditional values regarding early marriage and prejudice against women and other suppressions suffered by them. Briefly highlights the provision in the 73rd Amendment Act of the Constitution paving the way for women in decision-making at the grass root level. Discusses the position of women in Mizoram and poses some questions on the limited participation of women in politics.

Mohan, Rakesh. *Women and Development -- Need to Tap Full Potential and Capability of Women at Work*

Discusses the root cause of discrimination against women and the question of development of women in India. Studies the heterogenous nature of women on the basis of their social ranking/position in the family and work place. Notes the increase of the economic participation of women in two decades, upto the 1980. Observes the demographic imbalance of women during the period of 1901-1981, including Mizoram. Analyses the female mortality rate due to lack of proper health services, lack of education, less nutrition and their involvement in arduous activities. Emphasises on equal share to women in work force and to generate employment through the implementation of various programmes. Lauds the implementation of Programmes for Development of Women and Children and the role of voluntary organisations in Mizoram. Identifies the key areas, viz, education and health which still need attention in promoting the women in Mizoram. Further stresses on the need for the empowerment of women.

Lalmithanga, P. *Women's Development: Problems and Prospects*

An attempt is made to throw light on the importance of sharing equal responsibility by both men and women in human development. Appeals for rooting out prejudicial and discriminatory attitudes that hinder the development of women and children. While discussing the participation of women in all human activities in Mizoram, the author observes the deprivation of women from taking a leading part in the growth and development of the Church activities.

Noatary, K L. *Women's Development: Problems and Prospects*

Traces the historical background of the position of women from the early Vedic period to the emergence of the practice of *'Sati'* and *'Purdah'* till the rise of social reformation led by Raja Rammohun Roy. Further analyses the effect of promulgation of Constitution of India on Women's Development of the gender bias, awareness of the rights of women and women's development are the main aspects discussed in this paper.

Kumar, Vinod. *Women's Development: Problems and Prospects*

From the empirical study explored by the author it is found that society can prosper only when women are given an equal opportunity and their talents and capabilities are recognised. Further, the author maintains that man is not superior to women, that in fact they are complementary to one another. The writer also notes the discrimination women face both in areas of upbringing and education. He also raises the question of the privileges and rights conferred upon women by the Constitution of India and the laws of the land and states that it 'merely adorn the law books.' He appeals to the organisations meant for welfare of the women to be more realistic. The author contends that women's development can be achieved only if women themselves endeavour to protect and preserve woman's rights and ensure their welfare.

Lalneihzovi. *Mizo Women's Development, A Study of the Role of Mizoram Hmeichhe Insuhkhawm Pawl (MHIP)*

In this paper the author discusses the objectives and activities of the MHIP, a state-wide social organisation in Mizoram.

Chakravarty, P. *Women's Development: A Study of the Status of Mizo Women*

This paper dwells in detail on the esteemed position of the Mizo women. However, views the discrimination of property rights to women in the Mizo society which poses as an insecurity to women in case of the premature death of the bread-earner.

Prasad, R N. *Women's Participation in Politics and Decision-Making: Problems and Prospects*

Observes the limited participation of women in politics and their role in decision making. Discusses the factors that keep them from involving themselves in the political arena. Provides a number of suggestions for motivating and encouraging women to tap their potentials in this field.

WOMEN AND 73rd AMENDMENT ACT, 1992

Sub-regional Workshop on Panchayats under the sponsorship of the Rajiv Gandhiji Foundation, New Delhi. organised by Indian Council of Social Science Research - North Eastern Regional Centre, Shillong held in October 12 - 14 1995. The proceedings of the workshops are available in a book form, Power to People in Meghalaya, edited by M N Karma, L S Gassah and C J Thomas, (New Delhi, Regency Publications, 1998, p.180).

Lyngdoh, MPR, Women in Meghalaya and Constitution 73rd Amendment Act,* 1992 – *Problems and Expectations

Briefly discusses the vision of Mahatama Gandhi on the democratic participation of the people of India at the grassroot level. Outlines the amendments of the Constitution on decentralisation of power and the approval of the 72nd Amendment. Analyses the aims and objectives of the 73rd Amendment Act. Further, explains the concept of the traditional socio-political system of the people of Meghalaya. Highlights the role of various women's social organisations and Khasi women's participation in politics. Their contribution in different fields is also discussed. Finally stresses the need of a strong women's movement in the State.

Dutta, Niranjan. ***Panchayati Raj and Role of Women,*** (in Sub-Regional Workshop on Panchayats organized by Department of Public Administration NEHD, Mizoram Campus held in September 13 - 15, 1995)

Highlights the traditional system of the Panchayats during the Pre-independencera. Discusses the role of the *'village swaraj'* advocated by Mahatma Gandhi and the introduction of the 73rd Constitution Amendment Act, 1992. The author also focusses on some of the problems and prospects of involvement of women in the society. Finally, observes the urgency of women's participation in decision-making at the grassroot level.

Zatluangi, Veronica K. ***Panchayats and Prospects of Women's Development in Mizoram*** (in Sub-Regional Workshop on Panchayats organised by Department of Public Administration, NEHU, Mizoram Campus, held in September 13-15, 1995)

Highlights the role of Mizo women in the society. Gives a statistical study of women in government jobs, the number of girls studying in co-educational institutions and the increasing number of female traders at Bara Bazar, Aizawl. Observes the suppression of women in the society. A comparative study of the village council and panchayats is also dealt with. Finally, expresses support for the implementation of the Panchyati Raj in Mizoram.

Devi, L. Bino. ***A Constraint of the Political Development in Manipur: Meitei Women's Failure in Active Politics,*** (in Seminar on Constraints of Political Development in NE. India, organised by the Department of Political Science, Manipur University, Imphal held in March 21-22, 1988)

Studies the role of Meitei Women in socio-political movements, attitude of women towards politics and social problems leading to the failure of women involved in active politics in Manipur.

8

PROCEEDINGS OF NORTH-EAST INDIA HISTORY ASSOCIATION (NEIHA) IN DIFFERENT ANNUAL SESSIONS OF THE ASSOCIATION

Ghosh, Sujit K. ***The Status of Women in Barak Valley during the Colonial Period,*** (5th Session, Aizawl, 1984, pp. 127-134)

Highlights the historical background of female education and social participation of women in the Barak Valley and the role played by Babu Kamini Kumar Chandra in bringing an attitudinal change of the society towards uplift of women. The contribution of the Welsh Presbyterian Mission, the English Women Missionaries and Pandita Ramabai to the cause of female education in the Valley during the colonial period is also discussed. Projects the practice of child marriage in Tripura and the role of social movement to fight against certain social customs. Champions for the cause of the infant girls as advocated by Bipin Chandra Pal and Kamini Kumar Chandar in 1890.

Majumdar, Binapani. ***Status and Education of Women in Tripura,*** (6th Session, Agartala, 1985, pp 482-491)

Discusses the changing position of women as reflected in Indian History through certain periods of time. The deterioration of the position of women caused by traditional and conservative practice is also highlighted. Further, observes the impact of emancipation of Indian women after Independence in Tripura and also their participation in various programmes in the celebration of the International Women's year 1975. The author discusses the role played by the Tippara (Tripura) Hitasadhini Sabha for the cause of women's education in Tripura and notes the contribution of some renowned women in the field of literature, health service, music, dance, art, administration, games and sports and social services. Analyses the progress of women education in Tripura. Finally advocates for the encouragement of girls education in the rural areas.

Majumdar (Chaki), Binapani. ***From Tradition to Modernity: Changing Position of Women in Tripura,*** (7th Session, Pasighat, 1986, pp. 309-314)

Highlights some of the facts which brought the change in the position of women in Tripura.

Singh, N Joykumar. ***The Women's Movement of 1939 in Manipur.*** (8th Session, Kohima, 1987, pp. 338-351)

Presents the role of women of Manipur in the economic development of the state and women's movement in 1939. Traces the historical development of women's movement in India, and gives a detailed study of the women's movement in Manipur known as *'Nupi Lau'* for the betterment of the economic condition of the state of Manipur. During the British period, the movement protested against the British economic policy which degraded the contribution of womenfolk in the economic achievement in the state of Manipur. The active participation of women during the women's movement is also compared with the French Revolution in this study.

Sangkima. ***Position and Status in the Traditional Mizo Society.*** (9th Session, Guwahati, 1988, pp. 293-303)

Attempts to analyse the role of the family as an agent of moulding the social life of the people. Argues that the position of women reflects from the type of responsibilities held by her in the family in rural dominated society of the Mizo people. Her social participation also adds to her better position in the society. Observes the role of women as the backbone of the society.

Hluna, J R, ***Female Education in Mizoram.*** (9th Session, Guwahati, 1988, pp. 304-309)

Traces the background of education of women in Mizoram during the colonial period. Contribution of women missionaries in bringing about attitudinal changes among the Mizo is also reflected in this article. People's attitude regarding education to women is also discussed. Observes the participation of women in different social, economic, religious and political activities in Mizoram in the present scenario.

Lyngdoh, M P Rina, ***The Position of the Khasi-Jaintia Women as reflected in the Festivals and Dances*** (10th Session, Shillong, 1989, pp. 275-281)

Discusses the respectable position and role of women as reflected in the Lahoo and Nongkrem Dances during the religious festivals of the Khasi-Jaintia people.

Sen, Soumen. *Queens in the Khasi-Jaintia Tales: A Query* (11th Session, Imphal, 1990, pp. 58-62)

Gives a review of literature on the role of the queens in Khasi-Jaintia as depicted in the tales. Based on the historical value of oral tradition, the folklorist reviews the write-ups of the scholars presented in different seminars. Observes the significant participation of women in decision-making at the administrative level as women chiefs as portrayed in the folktales by the scholars in spite of their marginalization in decision-making in the society today.

Basanti, L, *Position of Women in Early Manipuri Society* (10th Session, Shillong, 1991, pp. 163-165)

Briefly discusses the role played by women in the political, economic, religious and cultural life of the Meiteis in the early society. Lauds the commendable participation of women in different fields. However, deplores the discrimination of property rights to women in this patriarchal society.

Goswami, V Pranay Jyoti. *Educational Development in the Barak Valley with special reference to Women* (16th Session, Silchar, 1995, pp. 290-298)

Analyses the growth and development of female education in Barak Valley. It also discusses the constraints of female education in the area and suggest remedial measures.

Gassah, L S. *Women, Their Participation and Role in Meghalaya Politics* (16th Session, 1995, pp. 299-306)

Analyses the participation of women in politics from the colonial period to the present political scenario of free India. The participation of women in decision-making as members of local durbars in Meghalaya is also discussed briefly.

Kalita, R C. ***Women and Agrarian Struggles in Assam: An empirico-historical approach*** (17th Session, Aizawl, 1997, pp.168-183)

Gives the historical background of peasant movement in Assam. Focusses on the participation of women in peasant struggle that took place in different parts of Assam before and after Independence.

BOOKS ON NORTH-EAST

Downs, Frederick S. ***The Christian Impact on the Status of Women in North East*** (Shillong, North Eastern Hill University Publications, 1996, p. 97)

Frederick S. Downs a renowned scholar from United Theological College, Bangalore, was invited by the Head, Department of History, North Eastern Hill University, Shillong to deliver the Professor H.K. Barpujari Endowment Lectures. Being honoured with the invitation, he took the opportunity to explore an area of interest and presented three lectures on the *"Impact of Christianity on the Status of Women among the Hill Tribes of North East India"* on the occasion, and hence this book.

The book contains three chapters dealing on the subject under reference. In his lectures, Downs made an effort to address some of the historiographical problems on the issues which he encountered during his research. In his analysis he looked from Christianity's contributions to social change to understand the situation in the pre-modern period, before the advent of the new religion. He reviewed some of the sources available on the subject from the missionary records of various kinds written by both men and women, administrative materials recorded exclusively by men and the works of social scientists. In his study he found that these sources differ from one another on the status of women in the pre-modern period which made him to direct his study to the work of theologically trained Christian tribal scholars who are women. Therefore, the first Chapter deals with the *Historiographical Problem*. Chapter II seeks to find an explanation as to why missionaries from Europe and North America became so extensively involved in female education. It also traces the connection between the nineteenth century Woman's Right Movement and the Protestant Mission societies that sent missionaries to the north-east hills to work among women especially in the area of women education.

Chapter III attempts to assess the impact of Christianity as brought about by missionaries upon the peoples among whom they worked especially regarding status of women. In this chapter, he limits his study to the two tribal groups, namely, the Khasi-Jaintias and the Mizos depending on the available sources. He also confessed his limitation and called upon the scholars belonging to the cultures concerned who have access to their respective tribe and language for testing the hypothesis developed for the study undertaken.

In the author's words, *"Though based on the extensive research, no one is more aware than myself of the fact that these lectures have barely scratched the surface of the subject. The hypothesis developed need to be tested by scholars belonging to the cultures concerned who have access to the language of each tribal tradition. I will have accomplished my purpose if I have aroused in the women and men who are connected with the North Eastern Hill University a desire to pursue the subject further - whether or not those studies support my own conclusions. It will be especially gratifying if women belonging to the tribes of the North east are encouraged to assess and define their own status in society, not being content to let this responsibility rest entirely with men. This will contribute, I trust to the development of a more egalitarian Christian Church and society in the North east".*

Fernandes, Walter and Barbora, Sanjay (Eds). ***Changing Women's Status in India, Focus on the North East*** (Guwahati, North Eastern Social Research Centre, Guwahati, 2002, p. 219)

The present book is a revised version of the papers presented at the National Conference, *Changing Women's Status, Focus on the North East,* organized by the *North Eastern Social Research Centre,* Guwahati, held on 11-13 October, 2001. Out of the eighteen papers, nine of them dwell on the status of women in India in general and the history of women's movement in South Asia. Half of them focus on North East India tracing the history of change among women till the present day.

The first paper deals with the introduction of the subject and provides abstracts for all the papers included in the present volume, followed by the paper on *Persisting Structures, Ideological Maneuvers, and Everyday Challenges, Reflections on Women's Movements in South Asia,* by Uma Chakravorti, tracing the origin of Women's movement with a focus on the Feminist Movement in India. Discussing about movements this paper maintains that the emergence of these movements emerged out of the different types of discriminations and forms of violence against women that women have to face in the society. Analysing various types of experiences faced by women which brought them to come together to protest against acts of violence on women, Chakravorti also throws some lights on the role of the urban and rural based women's movements. The Chipko Movement, internationally known for its eco-feminist perspective and the Bodo Gaya Movement are also included in this discussion. Concerned at the exploitation of women and threat to their livelihood, particularly the poor women, Chakravorti highlights the impact of globalization and its challenge to women's movement in India. In conclusion, she called upon the women's movement to bring change globally and to struggle for a less oppressive world.

Indranee Dutta in her paper on *Social Change and Women* discusses various theories of social change for empowerment of women. Talking about gender in- equality, the author elaborates on the need for evolving strategies that demand change in order to bring about gender equality in the society. She also outlines a number of steps for consideration to be taken by voluntary agencies and civil society to uplift the present condition of women.

Coming to the fourth paper, Kumkum Bhattacharya discusses the problems of women from a different perspective. Taking note of the trends in women's studies, she raises some questions of social conditioning and empowerment of women, arguing that women are capable of becoming the powerful agents of change only through the ways in which they can empower themselves in consonance with the kind of structures within which they function. Expressing her view on the women's movement, she appealed for the strengthening of the indigenous movement led by women like SEWA, and Chipko Movement, etc.

Dealing with personal laws, Flavia Agnes in her paper, *Minority Identity and Gender Concerns,* dwells on the history of law reform for the minorities with reference to the Supreme Court Judgement upholding the constitutional validity of the controversial Muslim Women's Act (MWA) and the amendment of the Indian Divorce Act framed by the Lok Sabha.

Looking from the economic point of view, Ritu Dewan, discussing on *Gender and Dominant Development Paradigm* attempts to analyse the implementation of the development paradigm which took place in India in the late 1970s, 1980s culminating in the 'structural' and Adjustment Programme of 1991. In her analysis, the author notes the overall impact of the programme implementation on major issues of concerns and its visible impact on the status of women in India.

Continuing with the development of women in India, Ilina Sen in her paper discusses on *The Impact of Globalisation on Women,* examining the impact of globalization on industry, agriculture and other areas of concern like WTO, violence against women, breaking down of the traditional social values, etc.

The above paper was followed by the presentation of Nafisa Goga D'Souza on *Development, Displacement and Marginalised Women.* Identifying the major indicators, the first part deals with development, and resource displacement discussing on land alienation, loss of common property resources, impact of mining, migration and its impact on women, and increasing atrocities against women. The second part of the paper studies the Development Project and Displacement of women. She also emphasizes on the urgent need of addressing the challenge of displacement and the development process within a gender perspective and the warrant for empowering women socially, economically and politically.

Viewing the threat from the new economic paradigm, Jennifer Liang in her deliberation in *Economic Development and Women* attempts to examine the role of women in the present context of market economy particularly in the tribal areas of the North Eastern States where women are actively contributing to the economy today. The author further raises the question of women being vulnerable to different types of violence in the prevailing law and order situation in the region. She further pleads for creating space for women in the present market economy by building structures to defend and promote the women through Self-Help Groups, Women's organizations, and movements like SEWA, formulating of women friendly policies and laws that support their participation and promoting of conducive industry and business. This paper also emphasizes the importance of local solutions through minor credit and SHGs with a view for bringing about policy changes.

Discussing the *Property and Women's Inheritance Rights in the Tribal Areas of the North East,* Jeuti Barooah seeks to understand the customary laws of the North East people, the right to inherit property and the role of women. This paper covers the Matrilineal Societies of Meghalaya, the Patrilineal Societies of Manipur, Mizoram, Tripura, Nagaland, Assam and Arunachal Pradesh. In conclusion, she suggests for the modification and codification of the customary laws relating to property rights and women in the changing social milieu.

Based on the study of six tribes from four states of North East conducted by the North Eastern Social Research Centre, Guwahati and St. Joseph's College, Jakhoma, the paper on *Modernisation and Tribal Women's Status in Northeast India* by Sanjay Barbora and Walter Fernandes, analyses the changes in the status of women with regard to their economic status pertaining to their access and control over the resources. The tribes under study include the Aka of Arunachal Pradesh, the Angami of Nagaland, the Adibasi and Boro of Assam and Garo of Meghalaya. It dealt with the issues of demography and women, higher education, low development, women and access to wealth, women and changing land relations, commercialization of agriculture, religious change and women's status. Observing the links between militarization and commercialization as being the hurdles towards the improvement of the status of women among the six tribes, Barbora and Fernandes encouraged development agencies and voluntary organizations to intervene on women related issues in order to bring about positive change in the region.

Monisha Behal in her paper on *Women's Collectives in Assam, A Short History of their Status and Present Day Realities,* presents a short history of women's collectives in the past and the challenges they face today. She also analyses the nature of women's work, their organizational abilities and the challenges that women's organizations need to deal within the present situation.

The paper on *Christian Marriage and Women's Issues in Assam* by Amit Kumar Goldsmith examines the institutional, cultural and traditional practices in the Christian societies of Assam with a view to identify the roots of the bias that exist against women.

The next paper is a study on *Matriliny and Education among the Garos* by Caroline R. Marak analyzing the status of men and women in the Garo society, and the changes that took place because of the contribution of Christianity and education especially to the uplift of the Garo women. In her conclusion, Marak calls for the Garos community to be open to a new set of values especially in economic activity.

The next paper on matrilineal society by Cerilla Khonglah discusses about the *Khasi Women and the Indigenous Question*. This work seeks to understand the question of the term 'Indigenous', tracing the origin of the Khasi people and the system of matriliny being followed by the society, the challenges that women have to face from within, the economic and social participation of women, as well as the position of women in the Khasi society. The author proposes for evolving a culture of gender equality.

Discussing on *Political Mobilization of Women in Nagaland, A Sociological Background,* Dolly Kikon highlights the history of Naga women from the colonial period, the unfavourable customary law of the Naga society towards women, the negligence of women in the Indo-Naga political conflict for more than half a century, the indifferent attitude of the society towards empowering women in armed conflict situations and in giving them a space in decision-making processes as well as recognizing their contribution in the peace-making process.

Dealing with *Changing Property Rights and Women's Control over Livelihood in Nagaland with special reference to the Southern Angami Hills,* Christian Kekhrieseno, in the first part of her study presents some basic information on Nagaland in general and the Angami tribe in particular. The second part examines the nature of the means of livelihood analyzing the occupational structure of the population. The last section seeks to understand the changes taking place in the traditional rights of women and its implications on women's status.

The last paper in the volume is, *Breaking the Myth: The Social Status of Meitei Women* by N. Vijaylakshmi Brara. Argues that Meitei women have a higher social status as compared to their counterparts in other communities in which they have a control over the market. Brara elaborates on the historical social resistance of the Meitei women right from the colonial period. She also briefly highlights the role of the women's group in the hill areas of Manipur. This paper also discusses the activities of the Meira-Paibis, the role of women at home, the position of working women, social norms laid down for women questioning the status of women in the Meitei society in the real sense. Finally, the author expresses the hope of change if women themselves seriously begin to tackle their own problems.

Fernandes, Walter and Barbora, Sanjay. ***Modernisation and Women's Status in North Eastern India: A Comparative Study of Six Tribes.*** (Guwahati, North Eastern Social Research Centre, 2002, p. 236)

This book is an outcome of the comparative study of six tribes of North East India conducted jointly by the North Eastern Social Research Centre (NESRC), Guwahati and the Department of Sociology, St. Joseph's College, Jakama, Nagaland. The present book contains seven chapters covering different aspects of the status of women in general, women in India and tribal women in North East India.

Introducing the study, Chapter One deals with the issues on *Changing Women's Status and Tribals in the North East*. This chapter begins with a brief background of the region and the recent changes taking place among the people and tribal women in particular. To understand these changes in the region, the authors start with defining the status of women in India and of the tribal women in the North East as the area of study.

Chapter Two focuses on *Methodology, Scheduled, Tribes, Villages* and *the Sample* carried out in the study. This study highlights the methodology used for regarding the choice of tribes, criteria for the choice of tribes and the tribes chosen. It also covers the profiles of the six tribes under study, the Adibasi, the Aka of the Arunachal Pradesh, the Angami, the Garo and the Boro. Further this chapter explains the objectives for choosing the particular villages and briefly gives the profile of each village selected for the purpose.

Chapter Three deals with *Demography, Education, Social Inputs and Women's Status* providing information on demography and women's status in term of the number of members in their family, sex ratio in the families, age group, sex ratio by tribe and the implications of the differences. Section two of the chapter discusses the social issues and women's status analyzing the factors responsible for determining the status of women with education as one key factor of change. On the other hand, examining access facilities, section three dwells on the aspects of access to drinking water, cooking and sanitary facilities. The data in this chapter presents the social and economic background of the six tribal communities.

Chapter Four provides the information on the *Access of Women to Wealth and Resources* highlighting different processes relating to occupational changes and control over resources, unemployment, land and sustenance, and agriculture. The chapter also analyses the related issues on land ownership and livelihood, land alienation, class formation, forest resources, and livestock. This chapter also takes care of the study of changing land use and land relation under which the issues of self-reliance and production and causes of food shortage reflect the major finding of the study.

Chapter Five elaborates the issues on the *Changes in Women's Status and Power.* This chapter raises the question of the attitude of women towards change and the decision-making power in the family relating to children and money matters. To understand the perception of power in the tribal society, Fernandes and Barbora studied the perception of women about their social reality from the question of their inheritance rights in the present and in the past. The section on changing role in the family deals with women's role in children's upbringing, decisions on children's health, women and children's education and marriage. The next section deals with women's role in the market economy in buying and selling of goods, and their control over the money.

Chapter Six expresses the views on *Language and Religion as Facilitators of Gender and Class Equity.* Observing language as one of the main factors responsible for attitudinal change in women's status, the writers discuss the role of language as a facilitator in bringing social change with regards to mother-tongue and the modernization process.

Considering the important role of religion in the life of the tribal of the North east this chapter includes a study on religion and women's status presenting the data collected from the respondents on religion with a discussion on religious change as a social process, followed by the analysis of the respondents' perception of social change, religious practices and gender justice, and the impact of conversion with a comment on the role of language and religion as facilitators towards equity.

Based on the context of the role being played by religious, educational and other institutions, chapter Seven gives a reflection on the possible role which these institutions can play in a movement towards equity as aspired by the respondents of the six tribes under study. The role of modernization, the role of institutions, women and social transformation, training of women, socio-economic changes and culture, the role of education, religion and civil society are the main agenda discussed in this chapter. There is an appeal to civil society, religious and educational institutions to come together to accept the challenge of the modernization process for the development of the tribal society.

Kaniampady, Elizabeth. ***Status of Women Working in the Tea Plantation (A Case Study),*** (New Delhi, Akansha Publishing House, 2003, p. 273)

This book is a result of the painstaking research carried out by the author, Elizabeth Kaniampady conducted in some tea plantations of Upper Assam. This work examines the prevailing status of women workers in Assam tea plantation in the context of the existing socio-economic condition to which they have been exposed since their emigration to this part of the country years ago. Introducing the study under investigation, Chapter One deals with a discussion on some basic concepts, review of literature, and the problem and methodology used in the study. Chapter Two on *Tea Labour* discusses about the land and people of Assam. It also highlights the origin of tea as beverage, briefly gives the history of the introduction and development of the tea plantations in Assam with a special emphasis on the various modes of recruitment of labourers in the plantation.

Chapter Three under the heading, *The Field* presents briefly the historical background of North East, and the land and people of Assam. The chapter also deals with the ethnic composition of the tea labourers in the two tea plantations in Dibrugarh and Tinsukia Districts. Chapter Four analyses some aspects of social life of the people in general focusing on the role of women in the society.

Chapter Five seeks to study the health and education among the women workers of tea plantations. It also discusses the factors having a strong bearing on the general health of women workers with regards to housing condition, environmental sanitation and quality and contents of food and drink consumed. The chapter further investigates the role of education among the tea workers, the literacy rate of the tea workers particularly women and the discrimination of women and young girls regarding education.

Chapter Six, dealing with *Economic Life* outlines the level of women's participation in economic activities and the problems they encounter in the process of their involvement. Focusing on *Community Life*

Chapter Seven discusses the role and participation of women in the community, particularly in the political sphere with special emphasis on the trade union activities. Lastly, Chapter Eight summarizes the entire work. In her concluding remark, the author calls upon the State Government, different women organizations and other NGOs to seriously look into the need of improving the status of women in the tea plantations.

Kar, Bimal K. ***Women Population of North East India., A study in Gender Geography*** (New Delhi, Regency Publications, 2002, p. 276)

The present book on Women Population of North East India, is a product of Bimal K. Kar's research work carried out during 1992-1999 in the Department of Geography, Gauhati University. This work comprises eight chapters with the Introduction. The aspects investigated here are the spatial patterns of demography and the social and economic characteristics of women in North East India. The study is mainly based on secondary data with primary data conducted in selected villages and urban areas for the purpose.

In the introduction, the author projects the overview of women population in the North East India in general highlighting the objectives of the study, the methodology adopted during the study including a brief discussion on Gender perspectives on Global, Indian and Regional context. Chapter two, *North East India, A Geographical Background,* covers the geographical and socio-economic background of the region. The *Demographic Characteristics of Women* are discussed in chapter three in terms of age composition and sex composition.

Examining the *Social Characteristics of Women,* chapter four analyses their literacy pattern, educational level, female mobility and pattern of crimes against women. Chapter five highlights the *Economic Characteristics of Women* with respect to women work participation, their occupational structure and the role of women in the economy. The next chapter, on *Status of Women: A Spatial analysis,* analyses the determination of status of women, population growth and development. The succeeding chapter elaborates the *Socio-Economic Characteristics of Women* in selected villages and urban areas focusing on the design of the primary survey, the demographic and socio-economic characteristics of rural women as well as urban women. The last chapter presents the findings of the study on women of North East India.

Mahanta, Aparna (ed). ***Human Rights and Women of North East India*** (Dibrugarh, Centre for Women's Studies, Dibrugarh University, 2002, p. 278)

This volume is a collection of papers presented during the two-day national seminar on *Human Rights and Women of North-East,* organized by the *Centre for Women's Studies of Dibrugarh University* and sponsored by the UGC and other agencies including NERC-ICSSR. There are 30 papers in the present volume. In her introduction, the editor Mahanta presents a brief account of the issue of human rights in the context of the conflict situation prevailing in the North-Eastern region for the last few decades, and how women encounter such situations. However, women's problem in this part of the country was rarely known earlier until the

Beijing documents highlighted these issues in 1995. To create awareness about women's problem in this part of the country, the Centre for Women's Studies, Dibrugarh University took the initiative to organize a seminar on the theme under reference for discussion and made an effort to bring out the proceedings in its present form for the interest of women, scholars and the society in general.

Papers in the volume have been thematically arranged in groups. The first group comprises three papers which deal with the general issues of Human Rights theories. RR Dhamala in her paper titled, *Human Rights and Women: The Indian Context* deals with the violation of human rights towards women in a male dominated system in India, in spite of a number of legislations to protect women. She further advocates for the better improvement of the women.

Archana Upadhyaya in her paper on *Woman's Rights and Human Rights: Perspectives and Perspectives* notes the international recognition of women's rights only after the U.N. World Conference on Human Rights in 1993 held in Vienna and in Beijing at the *UN World Conference on Women in* 1993. She analyses the argument on human rights from a third world perspective presenting the claims and counterclaims of an Enlightened Europe Universalism and the realities of religious and ethnic pluralism in the Third World societies. N.L.Dutta in her article, titled, *Human Rights and Women's Rights of North-East India,* traces the history of the struggle for human rights originating from Europe in the 18th Century and continuing into the 20th Century through the two world wars as seen in the right to self-determination of nations and the rights of the indigenous people followed by the *Universal Declaration of Human Rights,* 1948 and French Revolution. This article further examines the issue of human rights and women's development in post-independence India highlighting a series of employment related programmes with provision for women beneficiaries, legislations that seek to improve the working condition of women with a focus on the North East scenario on human rights and women. It also discusses the factors responsible for violation of human rights and violence against women. Papers on *Women in situation of Armed Conflict,* by Subhram Rajkhowa deals with the violation of human rights particularly the psychological problems faced by women in armed conflict situation. This paper strongly appeals for fixing responsibility upon police and armed forces in the event of any complaint of violation filed by women against them.

Similarly Roshmi Goswami, in her paper, *Women in Armed Conflict Situations The Need for a Human Right Framework* stresses on a comprehensive approach that needs to involve women to make them realize their economic, social and cultural rights besides civil and political rights. It also suggests some measures where women in armed conflict situation in North-East can play a different role in such a situation. The next paper on *Women and Armed Conflict Situation in North East,* by Indranee Dutta reviews the field study done earlier and provides some graphic case studies of women in armed conflict situations. Discussing on *Human Rights and the Women of Nagaland,* Neidonuo Angami observes the lack of awareness of women's rights among the Naga women in this male dominated society which is in a state of political unrest and where women are the worst sufferers in such a situation. She advocates for the coming out of women from their psychological and emotional mind set to express their protest against any form of violation of human rights meted out to women. Ksh. Bimola Devi, in her paper, *Women and Human Rights in Armed Conflict Situations in Manipur,* highlights the aspects of the U N Convention on Women's Right in the context of the different conflict situations faced by the women of Manipur and focuses on their role in social and economic activities in such conditions. Based on the personal interview, the paper on *Women, Law and Human Rights in Garo Hills of Meghalaya* by Caroline Marak makes an attempt to assess the state of affairs of the Garo, Hajong, Rabha and Koch women relating to their awareness about law and human rights as per the declaration of the UNO.

Afeefa Banu, in her write-up on *Women and Work: A Perspective,* presents the problems faced by women working in the teaching profession discussing the inequalities arising out of the social context.

M.D. Bhuyan in *Women and Poverty: An Aspect of Human Rights in India with reference to North-East India,* deals with issues relating to poverty and women participation.

The paper by Seema S. Singh on *Rights of Women Workers in Trade Unionism with special reference to the Tea Industry* deals with the study on the rights of women workers in trade unions in the tea gardens of Assam and evaluates the level of their participation.

Phukan, Minoti's article on *Working Conditions of Women Labour in the Tea Plantations of Assam: A situation analysis,* studies the problems faced by women labour in the tea plantations of Assam related to housing, maintenance, leave, maternity leave and benefit, medical and other facilities to women. Expressing concern at the deplorable condition of the women tea workers, the writer, suggests the intervention of the State Women Commission to improve the social problems of women in the tea plantations.

Ruplekha Borah and Mira Kalita. deal with the *Assessment of Physical Fitness and Drudgery of Assamese Farm Women.* Observing the significant role played by women from time immemorial in the multifarious activities at home and farming, this paper makes an attempt to assess the physical fitness of selected rural women in relation to the drudgery of home and farm activities.

Being concerned about women's right to health, Shiela Bora in her paper on *Medical Work for Women in North-East India: Role of the American Baptist Missionaries* dwelt on the initiatives taken by the American Baptist Missionaries to create health awareness and health education of the people in this part of the country. The other paper on health in this volume is on *Health Hazards and Human Rights of Nepali Farm Women in Kamrup District of Assam,* by Malaya M. Bora and K K Saharia. This paper seeks to study women's health problem with a focus on the socio-personal background of farm women of cattle farming community and the environmental hazards in which the farm women work.

Another article on *Women and Health: Problems of Adolescent Girls* by Nirupama Dutta briefly discusses the problems of adolescent girls in the Indian society. The other paper on health in this book is on *Reproductive Rights: Its Region Specific Relevance with Respect to India and the State of Assam,* by Mouchumi K. Borgohain. It outlines some of the aspects which figured in the discussion of the International Women's movement and its ratification in the Indian context. It also analyses the response for the implementation of the family welfare programmes in Assam. Rajput, Kishor Singh in the paper, *Safe Motherhood: A Human Right Issue,* discusses the various forms of discrimination against women in India and the health problems they face right from childhood till they reach their reproductive age.

Ahmed, Jasmine in the article *Health Status of Retired Elderly Females,* studies the physical status of the retired females after making the long journey from active labour to a well deserved retired life. The survey was conducted in five districts of Upper Assam.

Borkataky, Anju writing on *The Role of Governmental and Non-Governmental Organisations in Securing Human Rights for Women,* as a former member of the Assam State Commission for Women narrates her bitter experience on the political and the non-sympathetic attitude of the Commission in addressing real problems of women and suggests for the improvement of the Commission. The writer appeals to women organizations to take strong initiative to create human rights awareness among women.

Saikia, Monica, in *Wife-Battering- A Common form of*

Violation of Human Rights, discusses the different forms of domestic violence against women where the victims have to bear the trauma in their lives for the sake of their children. The writer as a General Secretary of the Legal Aid Cell of Sivasagar Zilla Mahila Zamiti and member of the District Women Cell highlights some of the examples of wife-battering that took place in the District. She outlines a number of Suggestions for creating a violence-free home to prevent the violation of human rights.

In the last paper Bora Talukdar, Daisy, on *Education as a Human Right and Educational Status of Women in Assam,* discusses the position of women's education in Assam making a strong note in the concluding remark, that 'education' is a human right which no one including women should be denied out of prejudice. Then only the status and rights for women can be recognized and achieved.

Ray, Ashok Kumar & Athparia, Rajendra Prasad (Eds). ***Women and Changing Power Structure in North East India*** (New Delhi, Om Publications, 2006, p. 256)

This volume is one of the publications of the North East India Council for Social Science Research (NEICSSR), Shillong, the outcome of the workshop on the *Changing Power Structures in the Tribal Societies of North East* India held in 2004. The volume comprises twenty three chapters focusing on the role and status of tribal women in the states of Meghalaya, Assam and Tripura in the course of changing economic, social and political institutions in the region covering the three states of the region.

Chapter One starts with the *Draft National Policy on Tribal–Does It Matter to the Traditional Power*

Structure?, by Ashok Kumar Ray initiating the discussion on a few important policy outlined in the Draft that affected the traditional tribal structures in different ways after Independence with reference to assimilation, doing away with 'primitive traits', preservation of distinct culture and oral traditions and interaction with outside cultures, minimizing tribal isolation through development of transport and communications, land, displacement and rehabilitation, shifting cultivation, research and women issues. E. Jyrwa in chapter Two discusses the *Changing Power Structure in the Traditional Modes of Education in the Khasi Land of Meghalaya* with reference to the role of women in the society. Another paper on *Changing Power Structure in a Matriarchal Society: A Case study of Khasis,* M. Sarikumar examines the major factors that brought changes in the role performance of the matrilineal and paternal relatives. The movement for change in the matrilineal system in favour of patrilineal specially in the matters relating to descent, inheritance and succession is also discussed in the present study.

In the following chapter, based on the secondary source of information documented by the British officials, Saifun Nessa in her paper on the *Changing Power Structure in the Khasi Society with reference to the Position of Women* dwells on the factors responsible for change in the Khasi society and power, the role and the position of women in the process of change. In chapter Five, Indrani Chaudhury and Saphimosha W. Blah question the marginalization of women in the political sphere in the Khasi society despite being economically empowered. This paper analyses the role of women in the traditional Khasi society, and in the changing scenario and also analyses the data collected on opinion based survey of men and women in urban and rural areas to find out their views about political empowerment of women. Chapter Six, *Political Participation of Women in Meghalaya–From Tradition and Modernity,* by M.P.R. Lyngdoh briefly' highlights the matrilineal system followed by the Khasi-Pnar and Garo people of Meghalaya and the traditional role of women in these societies particularly, Khasi women. Further, this paper discusses the political participation of women from traditional to modern times, elaborating the provision of the Government of India Act 1935, the right to vote for women, representation of women by reservation to State Legislative Assembly before Independence, as well as the election of women in post-independence particularly after the attainment of statehood of Meghalaya, to the Assembly and Autonomous District Councils. The impact of education on the attitudinal change of the society towards political empowerment of women, and the emergence of women's movement covering the profiles of the participation of women in electoral politics is also discussed in this paper.

Chapter Seven presents a paper on *Women Participation in the Society- An Analytical study of Core-Periphery Shillong* by Aurelia Badwar and P.K. Ryngnga. The study analyses and tabulates the data collected from 12 urban localities to find out the educational and occupational background of women. The role of women in politics and administration is also covered briefly in this paper.

In chapter Eight, the paper on *Constitutional Status to Traditional Institutions in Meghalaya: A Case Study of Khasi Society,* by B.P. Sahu views the tremendous process of transition in the Khasi society after the country's Independence in different fields of activities, the emergence of education, market economy and modern administration in the society. It discusses the traditional Khasi polity and the provision of the Sixth schedule in the state of Meghalaya. It also discusses the provision of the Sixth schedule in the state of Meghalaya observing the controversy between the District Council and the traditional institutions, the problems of the traditional institutions, the setting up of village courts and traditional institutions, the issues on land and participation of women in decision-making process of traditional institutions. Concludes with a suggestion to adopt a tier form of governance with at least one-third representation of women.

Chapter Nine, *Role of Khasi Women in Political and Administrative System–Tradition to Modernity* by Surojit Sen Gupta reflects the studies on women and politics in India and Khasi women in particular. He elaborates on the traditional role of Khasi women in politics and administrative matters, women and politics during British rule, the changing role of Khasi women and concludes with suggestions for encouraging Khasi women to participate in politics. In Chapter Ten, P. Devi presents a brief discussion on the *Socio Political Status of Women in Meghalaya.* Similarly, the next chapter by Gita Pyal on *Changing Status of Khasi Women in Society* highlights a few factors responsible for change in the status of women in the society in brief with special reference to the institution of the 'Khadduh'.

With reference to Garo Hills of Meghalaya, Chapter Twelve presents a study on *Women in Changing Power Structure in the Traditional Society of Garo Hills* by H.H. Sinha and G.P. Bhandari. Based on interview with the Garo intellectuals, teachers, people from towns and villages as well as the students of Tura University Campus, NEHU, the authors highlight the changes in Garo society as reflected in the Nakpate (Dormitory), Akin land or clan land, rituals, role of women, role of the mahari organization in the present Garo society, the current change of Garo community and the emerging environmental consciousness of the Garo women. The authors observe the positive changes taking place in the Garo society in favour of women. Anjan Jyoti Borah in his paper entitled, *Women in Garo Society, The Changing Trend in Socio-Political Life* examines the changing role of women in the Garo society on the basis of the micro study conducted in four villages of the East Garo Hills district, from the point of view of the traditional and present status of women, impact of Christianity and political awareness of women. Finally the study expresses hope for the improvement of the status of Garo women in the matrilineal society as indicated in the recent trend of development, particularly, awareness campaigns through education.

In Chapter Fourteen of this volume, Dwijendra Nath Deka, in his paper on *Changing Power Structure in the Traditional Tribal Society of North East India with special reference to the Role of Women,* discusses the trends of empowerment of women in the Bodo community of the Brahmaputra valley including a brief historical background of the Bodo people and the Bodoland Territorial Council (BTC). Chapter Fifteen presents the paper entitled, *Socio-Economic, Educational and Political Status of Bodo Women in the Brahmaputra Valley of Assam,* by Bijan Kr. Kunda. This paper is a reflection of the demography of North East region particularly the scheduled tribes population of Assam with a focus on the Bodos as the earliest settlers of Assam. The study delved into the socio-economic status of the educated Bodo women and their political consciousness. Finally, the author suggests for the gender sensitization of the legal system.

In chapter Sixteen, the paper on *Right to Development and Women in Dimasa Society,* by Alok Sen, drawing inferences from the light of Right to Development, the author attempts to investigate the real condition of the women in the Dimasa Society of the Cachar district of Assam from the point of view of the historical background of the society and the transformation processes which the society had undergone ending with a comment on the need for upliftment of women in the society.

The next Chapter is the paper by Sujata Bhadra, entitled *The Kocha-Rabha Women of Kalabari Village: An Appraisal of the Emerging Trends.* On the basis of the study carried out in Kalabari, the village in North-West of Kokrajhar district, this work gives a profile of the Rabha people with an elaboration of the empowering trend of women in the village with respect to their attitude, economic self-reliance, social participation, culture, etc. The study investigates the aspirations and perceptions of the women towards their day to day living. It also seeks to understand their problems and challenges in the society. In conclusion, the author suggests some strategic measures to enable women to face the challenges of life.

Mandira Datta Choudhury's paper on the *Changing Power Structure in the Traditional Societies– The Role of Barman Women in Barak Valley* throws some lights on the initiative taken by the D.N. General Assembly in tackling the problem of human rights in developing countries which had also contributed to the rise of global movement for women's rights. The aim is to understand the level of human rights awareness of the Barman women in Barak Valley and the changing power structure in the traditional societies. Observing the discrimination against women, this study suggests for gender equality that women in the Barman society could also get access to education, health care and other facilities for a better living.

C. Hazarika's paper in Chapter Twenty titled, *Women in Assam Agriculture–Focus on Programme Planning* studies the present status of women in Assam in agricultural activities and suggests a few programme measures for the advancement of women in recognition of their contribution in different fields of development of the society.

Chapter Twenty-one, *Women in Changing Economic Pattern of the Rongmei Nagas of Cachar,* by C.K. Biswas examines the status of Rongmei Naga women in urban setting of Silcher in the context of changing economy.

Chapter Twenty-two presents the paper on *Commonalities and Peculiarities among the Barman and Hmars Women in the Barak Valley,* by Pranay Jyoti Goswami. The study covers (a) Decision-making in household level, (b) Role of clan (c) Inheritance, (d) Village administration, (e) Education and Health and (f) Observation of festival. The study is divided into three sections. Sections I reflects a short history of both the tribes while Section II analyses the commonalities and peculiarities of the tribes in terms of women's participation in household decision, role of clan, inheritance, village administration, education, health condition and festivals. Section III gives the concluding observations.

Chapter Twenty-three, is the only paper from Tripura by Suchintya Bhattacharya entitled *Customary Laws and Participation of Tribal Women in Decision Making Process of Tripura.* This paper focuses on jhuming as an important phenomenon, customary laws relating to jhuming, laws of inheritance and the status of women, changes in the power structure. Lastly the author gives his observation and a strong call for empowerment in the true sense of equality between men and women to strengthen the social base of democracy.

Singh, Navinder K. ***Role of Women Workers in the Tea Industry of North East India*** (New Delhi, Classical Publishing Company, 231p., 2001)

Women constitute a major force in the labour market. The tea industry in India also have the women workers as the backbone of their industry where tea-plantations in North East employ women as pluckers in various gardens. The present book is a post doctoral study of Dr Singh on *Women Workers of Tea Plantation in North-East.* With the advantage of her association with the tea industry for 34 years by virtue of her marriage to a tea planter, she continued her research and was awarded her Ph D from the Political Science Department of Dibrugarh University.

This book contains six chapters. Chapter I deals with the introduction of the study focusing on women workers as tea pluckers, the origin and evolution of tea, tea in the National economy of India, and the tea growing regions of the world, and India, particularly the North-East India, Tea as a plantation industry, scope of the industry in India and the role of women workers in the plantations in the Third World countries. Chapter II presents the historical background and development of the industry in

North East India with special focus on plantation labour, and the emergence of the tea industry in India. The monopoly of the British East India Company of tea trade with China, the discovery of the tea Plantation in Assam, the problems of the tea industry in Assam during 1839-1870, *Labour Plantation Act* and other related issues pertaining to the tea workers, benefits and their basic amenities are dealt with in this chapter. Chapter III reflects the role of workers on Tea plantation who form a major labour force in the gardens. It also analyses the nature of women recruitment policy of workers in Assam Tea plantation, labour contracts and its abolition according to *Assam Labour Emigration Act of* 1965 and maternity benefits. Chapter IV on *Tea Plantation Women Workers as Social Forces and Community* examines the impact of women workers as social forces on tea plantations. Dealing with the urgency of capacity building of women workers, Chapter V studies the growth and development of political awareness among the tea gardens' women workers highlighting the factors responsible for the negligence, and exploitation of their ignorance of their right to development. Finally, in the last chapter VI the author gives the summary of her finding. Evaluating the future prospects of women workers on Tea plantations, she stresses on their capacity building so as to improve their prospects in the tea.

Sudhir, H and Hajarimayum, Jubita (ed). ***Violence Against Women in North-East India with special reference to Assam, Manipur, and Tripura*** (Akansha Publishing House, New Delhi, p. 140)

This present volume is a product of a three-day seminar organized by the Erema Gender Empowerment and Resource Centre, Manipur held at Imphal during 21st -23rd August, 2003, under the auspices of the Indian Council of Social Science Research, New Delhi. This volume examines the multifaceted dimensions of the situation of the region with special attention to the three states viz, Assam, Manipur and Tripura. The study investigates the various aspects of violence against women of this region with reference to structural factors, instances, trends, dimensions, impact, societal attitude, responses of the law enforcing agencies, etc. It also high lights some of the policy implications of the issue with valuable innovative ideas which will be of tremendous practical value to the social researcher's policy planners and activists.

In Chapter One entitled, *Note on Violence Against Women,* the contributor, Vasudha Gupta, seeks to define the concept of *'violence against women'* which has drawn the attention of the government and the society on the prevalent forms of violence against women, and which has also brought the international efforts to come together and address these areas of concern in various form. Addressing these sensitive issues she briefly highlights the situation of violence against women in India, with a focus on the legislative measures and legal rights of women, empowerment of women, the institutional mechanism like Department of Women and Child Development, National Commission for Women, Central Social Welfare Board, Rashtriya Mahila Kosh, National Institute of Public Cooperation and Child Development (NIPCCD), and the setting up of Parliamentary Committee on Empowerment of Women constituted to examine the measures taken by the government on women's security and equality. Further, the role of the NGO's, future programmes like the Action Plan for implementing the National

Policy for Empowerment of Women, the Enactment of Protection of Women from Domestic Violence Bill, 2002 to address the phenomenon of domestic violence, and the Drafting of Bill on Sexual Harassment at the Workplace as per the judgement and guidelines of the Supreme Court of India, to constitute complaint committees in all ministries/departments of both the Central and State Governments as well as the public sector undertakings to prevent sexual harassment of women at all working places. The bill being prepared by the National Commission for Women are also elaborated in this chapter.

In the next chapter, Archana Sharma and Indranoshee Das, in their joint paper, *Crime and Violence Against Women, The Situation in Assam–Trend, Dimension, Police Action and Societal Reaction,* attempts to find out the dimension and trend in the incidence of crime and violence against women in India and analyse the crime situation in Assam. Further, it examines the actions taken by the police in Assam in tackling crimes involving women highlighting a number of registered cases of violence against women and girls. This chapter has also expressed appreciation at the prompt response and action of the society particularly women organizations who protested against the heinous crime where a young girl was raped and murdered.

Dilip K. Medhi, in Chapter Three, on *Violence Against Women in Assam,* raises the question of inhuman and brutal acts meted out towards women and minor girls. He briefly discusses the different types of violence against women and expresses his concern at the rise of the reported and unreported cases of violence against women. Finally he observes the need of awareness programmes to reduce violence against women.

The succeeding chapter on. *Violence Against Women in Manipur,* by Esther Phinnu reflects the study conducted by North East Network (NEN) in Assam, Meghalaya, Mizoram, Nagaland and Manipur. The study observes the prevailing violence against women, and the areas of concern which needs to be addressed by the government and the society. Writing about the situation of the ongoing conflict in Manipur, the author notes with concern the rise of the various crimes against women and minor girls as reported in the news by print media which is viewed as the order of the day. In course of the discussion, the author also identified the issues that compounded the problems of women such as mental and physical health, HIV / AIDS, poverty and armed conflict situations. Observing the lack of political will to set up the State Commission for Women, she stressed on the urgent need of setting up the Commission to address women-related issues such as social stigma and ethnic clashes, displacement and gender inequality. Concerned at the plight of women in Manipur in spite of their contribution in the society, she further advocates for the participation of women in decision making and called upon the collective movement of women and women's organizations for the improvement and empowerment of women in the State.

In her paper on *Alcoholic and Drug Related Violence Against Women in Manipur,* Salem Irene attempts to examine the causes of gender-based violence, particularly meted out to the socially and economically underprivileged young women. Irene further expresses her concern at the rise in the number of girls and young men affected by HIV / AIDS who become the victims of alcoholic and drug user partner. Regarding the state of affairs of women in Manipur, despite the enforcement of prohibition the author observes there is continuing use of alcohol and drug in the state among all sections of the society particularly in the hill areas where liquor is customarily associated with traditional rituals and festivities. The result is the higher rate of HIV positive among pregnant women in the state. Highlighting the issues discussed during the Beijing Conference on Women in 1995, this paper analyses the survey of the International Institution of Population Studies on attitudes towards alcoholic related violence against women, and the issues raised by the International Centre for Research on Women where studies maintain that the majority of women face violence in their marriage. Lastly, to reduce alcoholic and drug related violence against women the author suggests some strategies through which women can empower themselves to fight against such type of violence against them.

Observing the plight of women as sufferers and the most affected lot in any type of conflict and aggression situation in the society, N Vijaylakshmi Brara in her paper, *The Seen and the Unseen Sociological Dimensions to Violence Against Women in Manipur* observes the increasing number of women organizations emerging in India who are raising their voice against the suppression and oppression of women. Dealing with women in Manipur, this paper studies the role of women organizations of different communities functioning in both the valley and hilly areas, the Maira Paibis, the Naga Women's Union, the Kuki Women's Association, Temkang Women's Union, Mojai Women's Union, Ghothe Women's

Union, Tangkhul Shanaolong and others. It also discusses the representation of women in Panchayat, Zilla Parishad and Legislative Assembly which is almost non-existent in this male-dominated society. Further it makes a critical observation of the disorganized functioning of the women organizations having no proper ideology to protect women against any type of discrimination and exploitation. Finally, the writer expresses hopes that educated women would take the initiative in questioning the present norms which are applicable only to women and the inhuman crimes against women in Manipur.

The next paper included in this volume is on *Violence Against Women in Tripura,* by Minakshi Sen Bandyopadhyay. This paper observes the low rate of crimes in general in Tripura compared to other States of India, but noted the higher crime rate against women in the State as recorded in the National Crime Board Bureau and by the Tripura Police from 1997-2002 as well as the cases registered in Tripura Commission for Women. It highlights the commendable role of the Commission in addressing women-related grievances in the State. In conclusion, the writer appeals to NGO's and general public to come forward and prevent violence against women. This chapter is followed by another paper, *Violence Against Women in Tripura: A Situational Analysis,* by Pramita Saha. The paper is divided into four sections. Section one introduces the topic and highlights the importance of undertaking studies and research on different aspects of violence against women. Attitude of women in Tripura towards violence against them is analysed in section two. Section three provides an idea about the extent of violence in the state on the basis of news reports.

Section four presents the interpretation of the findings.

Mishra, Kiran. *Women in a Tribal Community- A study of Arunachal Pradesh* (New Delhi, Vikas Publishing House, 1991, p. 95)

The volume is an outcome of the interest of the author, Kiran Mishra on the culture and institutions of different tribes of Arunachal. With support from the Indian Council of Social Science as a senior fellow affiliated to the Centre for the Study of Developing Societies he conducted a study on the role of women in the Mishing Society from the point of tradition and change.

Based on the methods of observation, personal interview, group discussions and questionnaires schedules, this book contains six chapters. The first chapter on *'The Canvas'* deals with the geographical, climatic conditions and historical background of Arunachal Pradesh, earlier known as the North-Eastern Frontier Agency (NEFA) bounded by Tibet on the north, Bhutan on the west, upper Burma now Myanmar on the east. The analysis reveals the embracement of the Buddhist religion by some of the Arunachal tribes inhabiting western Kameng, whereas those of the tribes living in the eastern parts like the Noctes were influenced by the Vaishanvism Sanker Dev. The other tribes follow their own traditional religion and belief. The history of Christianity in Arunachal Pradesh and the consequences leading to the Passing of the Freedom of Indigenous Faith Bill in 1978 to curb the threat of conversion in the state is also included in this chapter. The Arunachal people comprises of 110 sub-tribes belonging to about 20 major tribal groups spread in different parts of the state. The paper outlines the contribution of women in maintaining the traditional socio-economic art and crafts of these tribes. The author narrates how nature is reflected in their arts, crafts and domestic artifacts and lauds the skills imparted from generation to generation through learning by doing. He also outlines the changes in development that took place in the recent past in roads and transport, education, health services, electricity, public distribution system and other essential commodities. Other important issues discussed in this chapter are the awareness of the people on the importance of forestry, horticulture, land development, agriculture and crafts and the Maintenance Acts of 1975. Chapter Two highlights the traditional life of the Mishing. It also studies the family system and house structure of the Mishing society. Chapter three, *The Traditional Economy and Winds of Change* examines the Mishing traditional economy predominantly based on shifting cultivation, agriculture, tending and maintaining of mithun as their next main occupation and other supplementary activities like hunting and gathering food from the forests to meet other needs. The author also analyses the change in the land system of the Nishing society. The change which has taken place with the introduction of western education is also discussed. The change that took place among the Mishing community after the abolition of Slavery in 1955 which was followed by the introduction of permanent and settled cultivation forcing the government to restrict the entry of the migrant labourers is also examined in this chapter.

Chapter Four elaborates the profile of some Mishing women who shared their experiences, and explained their position and role reflecting the place of woman as the pivot of the home and society. The interesting part in this chapter is the analysis of the land relation and division of labour in the Mishing community where every member of the society work together irrespective of age or sex in different activities right from the domestic chores to the cultivating fields.

Chapter Five studies the customs, norms and rituals in the Mishing community with reference to roles of conduct and punishment, rituals and beliefs. Finally chapter six, on *Prospects of Nishing Women,* show that where women, in spite of enjoying a great measure of freedom and independence in managing economic affairs yet their role in the ritual, social and political sphere unfortunately gives the impression of being almost negligible with better opportunities in education and occupation however there is hope for improvement. The study notes the need for the modification of customary laws and the rights of women, and to create a better environment for them so that they can contribute significantly in different fields of social, economic and political.

Rao, V M. ***Tribal Women of Arunachal Pradesh*** (New Delhi, Mittal Publications, 2003, p. 222)

The book is an in-depth study covering various socio-economic dimensions of women in Arunachal Pradesh. It is an outcome of the project funded by the Tribal Development of Ministry of Social Justice and Empowerment, Government of India, New Delhi carried out by V.M. Rao, Professor and Head of Department of Research & Publication, Vaikunth

Mehta National Institute of Cooperative Management, Pune. The report of the Project which has come out in a book form is presented in ten chapters.

Chapter One discusses briefly about the tribal population in India and highlights the concept of Tribal Sub-plan introduced during the Fifth Five Year Plan (1976) formulated to facilitate monitoring of development programmes for Scheduled Tribes. It also covers the general discussion on the status of tribal women of Arunachal Pradesh which is a state inhabited by 25 tribes and about 100 sub-tribes. The chapter also outlines the objectives of the study, the methodology carried out for the purpose and the presentation of the Report.

Presenting the overview of Arunachal Pradesh, chapter two deals briefly with the historical background of the emergence of the state, highlighting the works of Verrier Elwin and other scholars. It also touched on the Anglo-Burmese War and the event of the Treaty of Yandaboo (1926), the position of Arunachal Pradesh as tribal areas of Assam, then, known as North-East Frontier Agency (NEFA), and other political and historical developments till the attainment of the statehood. Appreciating the accommodating nature of this area, this chapter outlines the demarcation of the international boundary popularly known as McMahon Line, the bone of contention in Arunachal between India and China that led to the Indo-China War of 1962. This chapter also looks at the rich resources of Arunachal comprising of flora and fauna of the State, the history and culture of its people, and their skills in arts and crafts. The natural devastation that took place in the wake of the great earthquake of 1950 and which has badly affected the entire territory has however been a blessing in disguise. It motivated efforts to develop the area in different sectors such as land, agriculture, forestry, livestock, industries, health, education, banking and credit, tourism, co-operatives and others.

Chapter three, *Developmental Programmes for Women* gives a glimpse of the implementation of the programmes aimed at the welfare and development of women in Arunachal with a review of the Integrated Child Development Services (ICDS) scheme, Integrated Rural Development Programme (IRDP), Development of Women and Children in Rural Areas (DWCRA), Mahila Swayam Sidha (MSS), Balika Samridhi Yoana (BSY), Udisha, Kisor Shakti Yojana and National Social Assistance Programme (NSAP) with a concluding remark about the process of implementation of the programmes.

Chapter four on *Profiles of Selected Districts* reviews the IRDP and DWCRA implemented in selected Districts with an emphasis on women. The study which covered Lohit District, Dibang Valley District, Lower Subansiri District and West Kameng District examines the progress in agriculture, horticulture, animal husbandry, paddy-cu-fish culture, hydro-electricity, livestock, tourism and gives a summary of the findings.

Based on the data collected from the target group, chapter five seeks to examine the marital and economic status of women, their age and educational level, size of the family, jhum cultivation, household income and sanitation with some concluding observations.

Further, to understand the contribution and the level of participation of women in day today decision-making, chapter six, attempts to elaborate on the work load and participation of women in decision-making, discussing the issues related to women's work, distribution of work load, exchange of labour and other factors.

Chapter seven relates the awareness of the respondents about local organizations, cooperatives, health care centre, anganwadi centre and Government loans.

Chapter eight, discusses the concept and the status of self-help groups in Arunachal Pradesh such as Alombro Enjuno Koronu Yakuchi Arne Akhamu (AKEY AA) SHG and the respondents' preference for SHG's.

Chapter nine documents the profiles of selected respondents. Finally chapter ten summarizes the findings of the study undertaken with a number of recommendations for the improvement of women in Arunachal.

Barooah, Jeuti. *Single Women in Assamese Hindu Society.* (New Delhi, Gyan Publishing House, 1993, p. 231)

This book is based on the doctoral thesis of the author, Jeuti Barooah from Dibrugarh University, 1990. This study of single women comprising of widows, divorcees and unmarried in the contemporary Assamese Hindu society was under taken to find out their problems and status in the society. The book is divided into three parts. Part One deals with the general introduction of the study and contains three chapters. Part Two with four chapters, provide the profiles of the Single Women and Part Three under the heading, Social Horizon of the Single Women contains five chapters. For further references, the book includes appendix, glossary, references, index and maps and figures.

Chapter one, the introduction investigates the status of women in the traditional Hindu society. It also review some related studies on women and explains the problem and the methodology carried out during the study.

Chapter Two, *Assamese Society and Women: An Outline,* discusses the issues about the Assamese society covering the socio-historical background, social network, and the place of women in the Assamese society and as well as the demographic perspective.

Chapter Three, *Guwahati: The Setting,* gives the setting (Guwahati) of the area of the field study undertaken, highlighting its population pattern and social profile of the city.

Chapter Four, studies the *Social Background of the Single Women,* from the point of view of their marital status, educational level, occupational status, income, place of origin and migration, and caste composition.

Chapter Five on *Single Status through Widowhood,* outlines and analyses the cases of widows in contemporary Assamese Hindu society and the factors that pushed them into the status of single woman referring to death of the husband, age of the woman at husband's death and duration of married life.

Chapter Six, *Single Status through Broken Marriage,* analyses the causes of being divorced and separated and the duration of their married life prior to that.

Chapter Seven discusses the factors for being remaining unmarried by choice and being unmarried due to compelling circumstances.

With reference to the *Social Horizon of the Single Women,* Chapter Eight deals with their living arrangements such as own house, parental house, rented accommodation, allotted quarters and hostels. Chapter Nine elaborates on the work situation of single women from the point of view of help and cooperation in securing job, nature of employment, income and expenditures, savings and investments, job satisfaction, work environment and adjustment of work life. Studying the social and cultural contexts of the Assamese society, Chapter Ten examines the role of the family and kinship structure as a whole in relation to a woman who is single with respect to the patterns of family households, patterns of kin relationship, friends and neighbours, religious activities, leisure and recreation, dress and ornaments, attitude towards marriage and remarriage. In Chapter Eleven, the author investigates the awareness of women about their rights as per the provision of certain legislations relating to child marriage, remarriage, maintenance after separation and divorce from husbands, and the legal provision under the Hindu Succession Act, 1956 for a widow to succeed to the share of her husband's property. Finally Chapter Twelve gives the concluding remarks and observations.

Das, Manjumala (Ed). ***Woman - A Collection of Assamese Short Stories*** (Diamond Jubilee Volume, Handique Girls College, Guwahati, Spectrum Publications, 1999, p. 269)

This volume is an outcome of the Diamond Jubilee Celebrations of the Handique Girls College. It contains twenty one English translations of the short stories of some writers who have made notable contributions to the Assamese short story from its inception. The theme of all short stories included in this volume is the portrayal of women characters in their different roles. Further, the short stories of this collection reflects the different aspects of the character of the woman in the context of the social, cultural, economic and the traditional background of Assamese society. This endeavour of the college will be of great use to the non-Assamese scholars interested on this area of study.

Sen Chaudhuri, Suchetra. ***The Bodo Movement and Women Participation,*** (New Delhi, Mittal Publications, 2004, p. 144)

This volume is based on the doctoral research of Suchetra Sen Chaudhuri submitted to the North-Eastern Hill University, Shillong. It is one of the thesis that the publishers themselves approached for publication of the work. The study which is divided into Five chapters seeks to investigate the silent involvement of women as leaders and able organizers particularly in the Bodo movement.

Introducing the study, chapter one briefly discusses the participation of women in social movements throughout the world. Further, it reviewed the rewriting of the past history of women's contribution to civilization by contemporary scholars from the 1960's to the French Women Revolution noted as the first wave of feminism, the Emancipation of Indian Women, the birth of women resistance during the Independence Movement of India, the participation of North-East Women in the freedom struggle, women's organizations formed in the post-independent India and women's movement in North-East India. The Chapter includes a brief historical background of the Bodo people and Bodo movement. It also covers the districts where the work was carried out and the methodology adopted for the purpose.

Further, *Introducing the Bodos,* chapter two deals with the review of literatures written both by foreign and Indian writers on the history and origin of the Bodo people. Discussion on the social organization of the Bodo, role of women in the family, law of inheritance of property, economic, religious and political organizations, the Bodo women in legends, marriage and separation, death rituals, participation of women in the festivals and their role in performing art are also included as the main areas of this chapter.

Chapter three, entitled, *Antecedents of the Bodo Movement,* traces the participation of the Bodos in various movements that took place in the past focusing on Sarania Movement, Moamaria Rebellion, the Brahma Movement, movement of Christian Missionaries, Tribal League and Tribal Sangha, Participation in the share Croppers' Movement of Assam, the Bodo Sahitya Sabha (BSS), Plains Tribal Council of Assam and AASU Movement and also Women's Participation.

Dealing with the *Bodo Movement and Women's*

Participation, chapter four investigates the details of the nature and magnitude of the participation of women in the movements. It briefly highlights the issues relating to the emergence of the Bodo Social Movement, the proposal of the nomenclature for homeland and other issues of the movement. This chapter projects the women's participation in the movement with special reference to women and mobilization, women and leadership, activities of women, women's organizational role, complexity of women's participation, women in Bodo volunteer force, role of AATWWF in dispute resolution and the formation of the All Assam Tribal Women's Welfare Federation. It also highlights the initiative of women in organizing seminars, conventions and conferences, and the role of Bodo women in literacy activities during the movement. The excerpt from the interview with Pramila Rani Brahma is also included in the present chapter. In conclusion, chapter five gives the summary of the findings of the study.

Ghosh, G K & Ghosh Shukla. ***Women of Manipur.*** (New Delhi, APH Publishing Corporation, 1997, p. 271)

Dealing with women of Manipur, the book first presents the historical and geographical background of Manipur comprising of different communities, the Meiteis settled in the valley and various tribes in the hill areas. The book is divided into 35 short chapters, and discusses the communities of Manipur, women's movement, marriage status of women, education, participation in festivals and art, inheritance, economic contribution and other related issues.

Chacko, Pariyam M, (Ed). ***Matriliny in Meghalaya: Tradition and Change*** (New Delhi, Regency Publications, 1998, p. 114)

This volume is an edited book brought out of a one-day seminar organized by the Department of Sociology, North-Eastern Hill University, with financial assistance from the Indian Council of Social Science Research-North Eastern Regional Centre, Shillong. There are ten chapters deliberated on Matrilineal Structures of the three major tribes of Meghalaya, Khasis, Jaintias and Garos in the volume reflecting the role of women in the matrilineal society.

Chapter one, the *Introduction,* briefly provides the composition of the State of Meghalaya and its people with an introduction on the matrilineal system of the Khasis including the abstracts of the papers presented during the seminar. In chapter two, *Matrilineal System: Some Structural Implications,* P M Chacko presents the theoretical concept of the matrilineal system in general. Juanita War discusses the concepts of the Khasi family and its structure and functions in the succeeding chapter. In the next chapter, Sohblei Sngi Lyngdoh throws some light on the historical background of the matrilineal system and the role of uncle in the Khasi society focussing on the aspects related to family fission, changing family, impact of Christianity and modernization and the future of Khasi matriliny. I.M Syiem in her paper on *Religion and Matriliny in Khasi Society, Some Observations* highlights some of her observations on matriliny, traditional beliefs and change, with suggestions for future research on the present area of study for more insights into the tenets of cognates and agnates, convictions, beliefs, rituals and practices in the Khasi society. O.L. Snaitang in his paper on *The Impact of Christianity on the Khasi-Jaintia Matrilineal Family,* examines the influence of Christianity on the Khasi-Jaintia *matrilinealism* in the pre-nineteenth century before its interaction with the modem agencies of change, the status of men and women, the cultural fragmentation in the Khasi society, the simplicity of the traditional culture, and changes that have taken place after the advent of the British. The next chapter is the paper by Philomath Passah who briefly discusses the changes in the matrilineal system of the Khasi-Jaintia family highlighting the roles of the youngest daughter and maternal uncle as well as the organized attempt for change.

In her paper, Aldila Mawlong examines some aspects of change in the family with a focus on the main factors responsible for bringing about change in the family system of the Khasis, including a note on the organization known as Syngkhong Rympei Thymmai, the organization campaigning for change. This paper is based on the field study conducted by the author in two localities, Mawkhar and Jaiaw, Shillong. Another paper in this volume is on *Christian Values Encounter Family in Meghalaya,* by Dominic Jala which covers the aspects of family in transition. It is followed by the chapter on the *Status of Garo Women in the Nineteenth Century,* by Frederick.C. Downs. This paper briefly narrates the condition of the Garo women as reflected from the literature based on the experiences of a woman missionary.

Lastly, this volume provides a *Select Bibliography* on the North-East, compiled by Pariyam M. Chacko.

Aleaz, Bonita. *Emergent Women, Mizo Women Perspectives* (New Delhi, Mittal Publications, 1st ed. 2005, p. 143)

This book is an outcome of the interest of the author on women issues who later conducted a field research on Mizo women. The study was carried out in Aizawl and Lunglei regions of Mizoram. This book has seven chapters presenting the analysis and findings of the author about the status of Mizo women in the process of social change and modernization due to the processes of education, and religion.

Chapter One deals with the background of the study and discusses the theoretical conception of social processes and the theories of modernization that transforms society with a focus on the situation of the Mizo women in the present society. This chapter also reviews the works of the western scholars, missionaries and the earlier administrative staff of the British government and of the tribal scholars themselves, as well as the publication of the Synod from Aizawl, on the impact of Christianity among the Mizo. It focusses on the emergence of the consciousness of Mizo women of their own right to decision-making process in the society. This chapter also provides the method of the survey carried out for the study. Further, it attempts to clarify feminist approach used in this work to assess the position of the women of Mizoram and it also covers the explanations of certain terms used in the present text.

Chapter Two, *The Women and the Within Structural Patriarchy,* studies the political history of the Mizo people in relation to the British period before the entire territory known as Lushai Hills came under the British rule. It focusses on the advent of Christianity and the resulting changes among the women within the patriarchal structure in the society. Based on empirical investigations on the circumstances that determine the changes among Mizo women, this chapter also discusses the initiative of the church in its emphasis on the role of education as an agent of change towards the progress and development of the society. The involvement of the women in the church is also highlighted in this chapter. It also discusses the codification and amendments of the customary law of the Mizo people known as Mizo Hnam Dan which was not totally favoured by the society inspite of the role of Christianity and education. Finally the chapter highlights the prevailing theological concepts within the structural parameters that influence the contemporary Mizo society depicting the situation of women in their active religious participation.

Chapter Three, on *The Extraneous Influence, The Growth of Organizations and Change,* discusses the position of the dominant sects within Christianity towards women in the West which influenced the institutionalized norms even in the eastern world including India. This chapter focuses on the nature of the Christian influence penetrating into the north eastern part of India, and gives a brief survey of some of the major women's organizations in Mizoram, which has brought about women's consciousness for change and development of Mizo women in the society. Finally, it assesses the nature and extent of organizational involvement by women from the point of view of the social, political and religious spheres as perceived by the respondents. This part of the chapter discusses extensively the activities of Mizo women organizations committed to the development and welfare of women as the prime determinants of change.

Chapter Four, *The Women, the Church and Change,* dwells on the impact of Christianity which acts as a prime agent in bringing about change in the outlook towards women. Chapter Five, *Tradition, Modernity and Change* explores the inter-connection between culture, tradition and change, repeating the significance of traditional institutions and practices; and the perceptions of the respondents of the position of women in traditional institution and finally focusing on indigenization within the church. This chapter also reviewed some of the literatures related to North-Eastern India seeking to resolve the dilemma between tradition and change in the tribal context.

Based on the work of the Nobel laureate Amartya Sen and Jean Draze (1995; 1996) who emphasized on the linkage between socio-economic deprivation and lack of personal freedom, Chapter Six, *Education, the Economic and Decision-making* reiterates the argument on correlation between literacy and empowerment of women in general with a focus on the Mizo women. This chapter also discusses the issues on economic structure– - women and inheritance, the rural structure, and supplementing income by nonagricultural occupations. Finally, Chapter Seven gives the summary and conclusion of the study.

Vitso, Adino. *Customary Law and Women-The Chakhesang Nagas* (New Delhi, Regency Publications, 2005, p. 106)

The present book is the outcome of the doctoral thesis of Adino Vitso, entitled, *Customary Law and Women-*

The Chakhesang Nagas. The book is divided into six chapters.

Chapter one, attempts to define the term 'law' and the status of women in general. It introduces the Chakhesang women and gives a note on the influence of the customary law on the women. The next chapter deals with the land and people of Nagaland discussing the history of Naga people in general, their language, religion, the impact of British rule on Naga customary laws, the Chakhesang Nagas, the Khezhakeno village with a focus on the important sites in the village, historical importance of the village and the village organization. The succeeding chapter, *Customary Law* elaborates the important role of the customary law in traditional system of village administration, the present system of village administration, customary laws and practices related to agriculture, changes in customary law, domestic laws and rituals, rite-de-passage, observation during the pregnancy of women and marriage, death, dress and ornaments and food. While chapter four, *Customary Law and Women* dwells on the social status of women, marriage and divorce, economic and political status, inheritance of property and concluding remarks. This chapter is followed by the presentation dealing with *Continuity and Change* in the customary laws relating to the life of women. The discussion in this chapter includes the issues on domestic and social position of women, marriage laws and customs, place of women in the village administration and concluded with a note on the role of education and Christianity as the main factors which brought about changes in the customary law regarding women. Finally, chapter six summarizes the findings and observation of the study.

Nath (Bhowmik), Krishna. ***Status and Empowerment of Tribal Women in Tripura*** (Delhi, Kalpaz Publications, 2001, p. 217)

This book analyses the social, economic, marital and economic status of tribal women of Tripura with an attempt to describe the obstacles that come in the way of their empowerment. The work contains five chapters.

In the first chapter, this study briefly traces the historical background of the tribal women of Tripura drawn from the days of Royal. A chart of growth of the tribal population of Tripura is provided based on the Census Reports 1931-2001. The women in ancient Indian culture particularly the upper class were learned women and enjoyed a high status. Chapter two, *A Glimpse of Tribal Women in Royal Families of Tripura,* expresses concern at the gradual deterioration of the status of women caused by the foreign invaders. This chapter includes profiles of the tribal women in Royal Families of Tripura. Chapter three discusses the social, economic, marital and religious status of the common tribal women of Tripura, the Reangs, Jamatia, Chakma, Garo, Kuki, Mao, Lushai and Halam women. Chapter four gives the summary of the study. Lastly, chapter five projects the Gazetted Women (S T) officers who belong to the four major tribes of Tripura.

MONOGRAPHS

The monographs included in the present annotated *Bibliography* are the special projects of *Women in Security, Conflict Management and Peace (WISCOMP)* awarded to the scholars under the *Scholar of Peace Fellowships* designed to encouraged original innovative work by academicians, policy-makers, defence and foreign affairs practitioners, NGO workers and others.

Banerjee, Paula. *Across the Experiences: Naga Women in Sri Lanka* (New Delhi, WISCOMP, 2003, p. 26)

The monograph is the product of a special project of the WISCOMP given to Paula Banerjee in 2000-2001, titled *Women's Network for Peace.* This work is a documentation of a dialogue at work between women from two conflict zones across South Asia–Nagaland and Srilanka. It consists of the proceedings of the workshop in Sri Lanka held in January 2001 and addresses questions of how to strengthen women's initiatives for peace in situations of conflict.

Khala, Khatoli. *The Armed Forces (Special Powers) Act and Its Impact on Women in Nagaland* (New Delhi, WISCOMP, 2003)

This monograph emerged out of the academic project undertaken by Khatoli Khala sponsored by the *Women in Security, Conflict Management and Peace (WISCOMP)* in the year 2000-2001. The work examines the impact of the Armed Forces Special Powers Act and the violation of human rights of women in Nagaland over the last 52 years. The author analyses the cultural, socio-economic and political aspects of the situation in Nagaland which led to the imposition of AFSPA. It also seeks to provide a guide to prevent incidents of such human rights violations in the state.

Kikon, Dolly, *Experiences of Naga Women in Armed Conflict, Narratives from a Militarized Society.* (New Delhi, WISCOMP, 2004)

This monograph is the outcome of the projects of the WISCOMP, conducted by Dolly Kikon. The study interprets a series of narratives drawn from Wokha, Kohima and Dimapur Districts of Nagaland portraying the experiences of Naga women in a violent conflict situation. In her analysis, the author also looks at the militarization and marginalization of Naga women in the social, political and economic fields and the legal and continuing dialogue between the Naga people and the State functionaries.

Takhellambam, Bhabananda. *Women's Uprising in Manipur, A Legacy Continued.* (New Delhi, WISCOMP, 2003, p. 45)

The monograph is the result of an academic project undertaken by Bhabananda Takhellambam who was awarded the *Scholar of Peace Fellowships* by the *Women in Security, Conflict Management and Peace (WISCOMP)* in the year 2000-2001. This work traces the role of the women's Meira Paibi Movement in Manipur in the context of the rise of the separatist movement and the imposition of the Armed Forces Special Powers Act of 1958. Based on interviews with the women activists and the author's personal insights, the work gives a glimpse into the Manipuri society, its complex past and its current problems.

Women Development, A Special Emphasis on Rural Women. This monograph is an outcome of the seminar organized by the State Institute of Rural Development, Meghalaya as a part of the Celebration of Women Empowerment Year, 2001 during 29-30 October, 2001 held at Nongsder. This monograph contains six papers.

M P R Lyngdoh in her paper on *Political Participation and Empowerment of Women in Meghalaya* stresses on political empowerment of women in the legislatures and in the local political institutions. She observed that women participation in politics showed a downward trend since the days when women participated in the resistance movement against the British under U Tirot Singh. Wider representation of women in the decision- making bodies will enable them not only to share power but more so to speak for themselves so that women's priorities can be properly taken care of.

The second paper on *Rural Women and Environment in Meghalaya - A Glimpse,* was presented by C. Khonglah. Her paper observes that participation of women in various social activities to keep the environment clean and green for sustainable development is always silent and therefore is always not visible. While womenfolk in the rural areas are involved in tedious works yet no serious efforts have been made to conduct study and research related to rural women and their affinity to environment, she asserted. She also highlighted aspects such as health, employment generation, decision-making, and marketing skills as having direct bearing upon women empowerment.

The next paper on *Importance of Functional Education in the Context of Rural Development,* by Mrs. B. K. Sangma points out that education is an important instrument for social change and vital for socioeconomic advancement. She shows concern at the number of dropouts and she calls upon everyone to work for the betterment of the society.

In her paper on *Government Initiative towards Women Empowerment,* L.R. Sangma highlights some of the major programmes initiated and implemented by the Government such as Swayamsiddha, Kishori Shakti Yojana and Balika Samridhi Yojana. This paper throws some light on opportunities for women to access themselves to various facilities in order to enhance their livelihood. She also stressed on the active participation of women and appealed for organizations to come forward and take part in the programmes for the sake of rural women.

The paper on *The Status of Khasi Women - Status, Rights and Power* by S. Rynjah focusses on the status, rights and power of the Khasi women as envisaged in the customs and usages. She hope that through the process of empowerment women will be further strengthened with the inherent rights and status already enjoyed by them. This will definitely activate women especially in the rural areas to come forward to take active part in the process of development, thereby enhancing their contribution to the economy.

Lastly the paper on *Access of Legal Awareness to Women* by Minoti Sharma points out that ignorance of law is no excuse that every citizen is supposed to know the law of the land. A law breaker will be punished irrespective of status or position. The writer stresses that the government should take steps to institutionalize a legal awareness scheme to provide legal literacy to women in particular and the society in general. She emphasizes that only through knowledge of law women could become empowered enough to fight against injustice and thereby lead a life with human dignity.

AUTHOR INDEX

■■■